Secrets of

GRACE

Uprooting Condemnation, Guilt, and Fear

Special Thanks

I would like to thank my wife Joyce, who has stood by me all these years in ministry. She has not only been my greatest encourager, but also my best friend. I would also like to thank my kids, Jason and Jamie, who have been such a blessing in our home. Special thanks to my parents, Jack and Patty. May the Lord richly bless you for all your love and support you have given me all these years.

Secrets of GRACE

Uprooting Condemnation, Guilt, and Fear

JACK HOLT

Introduction

There are times in ministry one never forgets. I'd like to tell you about one of those times. I had been teaching on the subject of the goodness of God, and after one particular service a woman came up to me and said, "Pastor, I love what you preached." I told her thanks, but then she said something to me I will never forget. She said, "It seems like Jesus is too good to be true!" I responded to her by saying that he's a whole lot better than I'm able to articulate. Needless to say, throughout all these years I have discovered that he is indeed far greater than I ever thought he could be. It's because of his grace. I believe the gospel of grace, once understood, releases a measure of God's goodness over people's lives that changes them forever.

I want to give you a warning, though, before you read this book. If you desire to remain the same, don't bother reading any further! On the other hand, if you are looking for a positive change in your life, then jump in with all your heart and feed on the wonderful truths waiting for you.

Uprooting Condemnation, Guilt, and Fear

TABLE OF CONTENTS

Chapter 1
Believing in Winning Again

Everyone needs a winning spirit. The scriptures call this the spirit of faith.

Over the years I have seen many wonderful people who had lost that "slide in their glide;" they'd lost the joy of their salvation and were no longer excited about their future. What is it that causes us to run with prairie dogs instead of run with the lions? What is it that causes us to cluck with the chickens instead of fly with the eagles? What is it that causes us to drink from ponds rather than drink from springs? God created us for greatness; He did not create us for defeat! God created us to prevail, not to be preyed upon. He created us for peace, not depression; for health, not sickness. He created us for increase, not decrease in our lives. I believe the cause of this thinking comes from an underlying current of condemnation.

Romans 8:1, 4
"There is therefore now no condemnation to those who are in Christ Jesus. Who do not walk according to the flesh but according to the Spirit."

"...that the righteous requirement of the law might be fulfilled in us who do not walk according to the flesh but according to the Spirit."

In the Greek text, the phrase *who do not walk according to the flesh, but according to the Spirit*, is only written once, which is originally found in verse four. The translators took that phrase from verse four and also placed it at the end of the first verse. I personally believe they did this because they just couldn't grasp the truth that there is no condemnation without any conditions. Literally, verse one reads like this:

"There is now no condemnation for those in Christ Jesus."

Period.

You might be saying, *Why are you making a big deal about this?* I am for one reason: because there are no conditions to freedom from condemnation except to believe on Jesus.

Think about it for a moment. If you believe the only time you are free from condemnation is when you are "walking in the Spirit," you are going to be under condemnation during most of your lifetime. When you get angry on the freeway, you'll be under condemnation; when you're upset with your spouse, you're going to be under condemnation; when you lose your temper with your kids, you're going to be under condemnation.

Condemnation creates a negative expectation in your life. Here's an example of this kind of condemnation at work. You go to court and you're found guilty of a crime, and the judge says that he'll pronounce a sentence upon you within 30 days. So, for the next 30 days you do not have a good expectation of the future, but an expectation of the future filled with hardship and pain. It's very hard to develop a winning spirit if you are expecting bad things to happen to you.

Condemnation Doesn't Exist

Remember how Romans 8:1 begins? It says, "There is now no condemnation . . . " This means that it doesn't exist any longer in the believer's life. On the cross, Jesus became sin for us and was condemned on our behalf. Every sin you would ever commit was placed upon him; therefore God brought all of His condemnation and wrath upon Jesus.

There is no more condemnation or wrath concerning your sin because God the Father unleashed it all upon Jesus. Whenever you feel condemned, understand that it is a lie—an illusion. Condemnation doesn't exist for those who have put their trust in Jesus.

Continuing to walk around with a spirit of condemnation once you're a follower of Jesus is like being on a deserted island where it appears as though there's no fresh water to drink. Imagine you were on this deserted island, but see a well filled with what looks like fresh water. The only problem is there's a sign on it that reads POISON. What you didn't know was that there's a farmer nearby who put that sign on the well because he doesn't want to give you any of that fresh water! Have you ever seen homes with signs that say BEWARE OF DOG yet they have no dog at all, or the one they have is harmless? These are just examples, but the principle is the same: Satan lies to people because he doesn't want them partaking in the blessings of the Lord. If Satan can keep you thinking like a loser instead of a winner, then it will be hard for you to win at life.

Let's examine Romans 8:1 one more time:

"There is therefore now no condemnation to those who are in Christ Jesus."

I love the phrase "in Christ." Once you get "in Christ," there is no return ticket. It's like a one-way road or like a turnstile at a coliseum that's only used for getting in, not going back out. The reason why we're secure in Christ is because he paid for our salvation and he holds it together by his faithfulness, not ours. Praise be to God!

Can Sin Stain Your Robe?

Once condemnation has been taken away from us, the gift of righteousness is given to us in its place. The scriptures describe the gift of righteousness like a robe; like a very special kind of robe. Whenever my wife buys me clothes, she always tells me not to work on the car or paint with my good clothes on. I tried to get around this once by purchasing water-based paint instead of oil-based paint, thinking I could paint with my good clothes on. I tried to be careful, but I spilled some paint and tried cleaning it out. Well, it didn't come out and I ended up facing the music with my wife!

The good news is that the robe of righteousness Christ gave us is "stain proof," no matter how many times we may make mistakes. The truth is that our robe of righteousness remains as white as snow, for it wasn't our obedience that earned us that robe, it was Christ's obedience. The devil loves to deceive us into thinking the sins of the past have stained our righteousness. If we believe this, we'll feel unworthy to receive all that God has for us. If we believe our robe is full of spots and blemishes, then we might not have a desire to sit up front in church from where the blessing flows, but maybe we'll sit in the back feeling like we can't receive the great blessings God has for us. I want you to know you're looking good and your robe of righteousness has no blemish or spots at all. Remember, Christ's obedience earned it for you!

Rightly Dividing the Word

One of the reasons we feel condemned or unworthy at times is because we do not rightly divide the Word of God. Misinterpretation of scripture is largely due to inaccurately discerning—or dividing—covenant law and covenant grace. If we take, for example, Old Testament verses and apply them in the exact same way to today, we begin treating people who are born again as if they are still spiritually dead. All the saints of the Old Testament were dead in their trespasses and sin; it wasn't until after the resurrection of Christ when people could be born again and made spiritually alive. As the body of Christ, we must heed the words of Paul regarding this very important mandate.

> *2 Timothy 2:15*
> *"Be diligent to present yourself approved to God, a worker who does not need to be ashamed, rightly dividing the word of truth."*

The Teachings of Jesus

Sometimes we view some of Jesus' teachings which he taught under the law and try to apply that teaching to grace. Let me show you here through this next example by looking at the following scriptures.

> *Matthew 6:14, 15*
> *"For if you forgive men their trespasses, your heavenly Father will also forgive you, but if you do not forgive men their trespasses, neither will your Father forgive your trespasses."*

If you look at the context in which Jesus is speaking, you will see it is an Old Testament prayer. In the previous verses you will find the Lord's prayer and within it there's no mention of the name of Jesus. After the resurrection, Jesus' name was exalted above every name. Under grace people began to receive from God based on the work of Jesus, not based upon their own works.

Jesus' teaching was done while he was under the law, in the process of fulfilling it. He was preaching directly to those under the law. Therefore, very little of the truth he preached was directed to the church to come, which would be born after his resurrection and the outpouring of the Holy Spirit. Consider his sermon on the mount (Matthew 5-7). That was a sermon certain to bring people to the end of themselves concerning the law. Jesus said things such as, "...be perfect, just as your Father in heaven is perfect." How could anyone accomplish this? He also said (to paraphrase) to pluck out your eye or to cut off your hand if it offends you. He was talking about the religious leaders of his day who believed they could keep the law, but proved that it was an impossible task. He revealed that they obeyed outwardly but were inwardly corrupt.

> **"This is the power of the lie of condemnation: it keeps people from believing they are worthy to receive God's blessings. In the spirit realm, for those who trust in Jesus, condemnation no longer exists, but if you operate as if you are still condemned, then that belief affects your reality, the one in which you are living right now."**

When you do not rightly divide the Word, you start thinking like someone under the law. Under the law, you must do something in order to be blessed. Under grace, you believe something in order to receive blessings. Let me share with you another example. When you gave your life to Christ, did you come forward to the altar and say, *Lord, I'll go out and make right all the wrongs I had committed against people first, then I'll come back and you can forgive me for all my sins*? Of course not! You were forgiven the moment you believed in Jesus as your Savior.

Many people go through life with a spirit of condemnation. These are people who wish they could have corrected a wrong, but were unwilling or unable to do it, and that prevents them from really believing they can receive God's best. Take, for instance, a person who is unwilling to reconcile with a friend. Or perhaps a person who has experienced a lot of anger toward his or her parents; those parents died without their child reconciling with them, and that causes a lot of regret for that person. Again, this type of thinking causes many people to stay in a place where they feel condemned and can't receive God's best.

I know of some people who believe they can only receive forgiveness if they "stay on top of it." In other words, they carry around a careful list of sins they've committed, and make sure they ask for forgiveness for all of them. If we had to go around carrying that burden, who do you think would reach heaven? What about all those sins that may have been forgotten? Most everyone would be dying in their sins if that were the case. Nobody—and I mean nobody— goes to heaven if they have sin in their lives.

This is the power of the lie of condemnation: it keeps people from believing they are worthy to receive God's blessings. In the spirit realm, for those who trust in Jesus, condemnation no longer exists, but if you operate as if you are still condemned, then that belief affects your reality, the one in which you are living right now.

> *Hebrews 10:14*
> *"For by one offering He has perfected forever those who are being sanctified."*

How long is forever? Isn't it forever and ever? Through Jesus' perfect sacrifice we are made in perfect standing with God.

Condemnation Kills Faith

Let me show you how condemnation causes you to expect negative outcomes. In the Bible, God had called the first generation of Israelites out of Egypt to go into the promised land. The scriptures tell us they refused to mix their faith with God's promises. It also says that God swore in His wrath that none of those over 20 years old would go into the promised land, and instead they would wander in the wilderness for 40 years and die there. The truth is that those people were under the law at that time.

Grace was given to us when God had placed His wrath upon Jesus at the cross.

Think about how the children of Israel must have felt—all those twenty years old and over. Now they no longer expected to have the blessing of long life which God had promised. They must have figured they would die in their sixties if they were around 20 years old at the time God pronounced judgment on them. Now they could not expect to drink from wells they hadn't dug, or to move into homes they hadn't built, or tend to the farms and vineyards they hadn't cultivated, for again, these were promises made to those who were to possess the promised land. The children of Israel 20 years and older could only develop a negative expectation of their outcome because of God's condemnation upon their lives.

If God removed that condemnation through Jesus, then we should be expecting good, not evil; long life instead of a short life; health instead of sickness. We should expect increase in our lives, not lack.

How Does God Judge Us?

God never judges us by punishing us for something we've done. He judges us by correction so we can maintain His blessings, not only in this life, but in the life to come. In the letters to the seven churches found in Revelation, Jesus examined all of the works of those churches. To most of the churches he tells them if they overcome, they will receive eternal rewards. To one church he says they will partake of the tree of life in paradise. To another church, he says if they overcome, he will set up a throne for them like his Father set for him. He even says they will rule with a rod of iron. Jesus was referring to rewards and reigning with him in the life to come. Even when he admonishes the lukewarm church, he does so by telling them to repent so that they would not lose what they had obtained through faith. Please don't miss this point: If we do not see God's judgment toward the church in the right light, it will kill the winning spirit within you.

Light Drives Out Darkness

Let's now look at another scripture that will help you keep this winning mindset.

Colossians 1:12
"...giving thanks to the Father who has qualified us to be partakers of the inheritance of the saints in the light."

I want to show you a couple of things about this verse. First, it says Jesus has qualified us; we do not qualify ourselves. Second, it says that we are in the light. The last time I checked, whenever a light is turned on it drives out the darkness; the darkness is no match for the light. I am showing you truth to shed light on these dark areas in your life so you can walk in the dominion God has given you in Christ Jesus. Darkness never drives out light, but light always drives out darkness. Right now as you're reading this wonderful truth, the light is driving out the devil's lies concerning condemnation.

When you awaken to righteousness in your life, it will drive out the negative expectation of defeat. The truth of God's word will drive out the lies of the enemy which thrive in darkness. The more you become established in the truth concerning righteousness, the more you are able to drive out all negative expectations. If you're married, stop expecting your marriage to get worse instead of better. If you chronically worry about your health, stop expecting your health to get worse instead of improving. Stop expecting less and begin expecting more in your life!

Once Christ qualified us for all these blessings, it was no longer about what we can earn; instead it became about what we desire in our lives. For example, let's say you are looking to buy a house. When you visit the real estate agent, he begins to ask about how much money you make and about your credit condition, and then shows you houses based on what you can afford. Unless you have lots of money there will be certain parts of town that you won't consider simply because you can't afford the homes there. Suddenly, Jesus shows up and tells the agent he wants the financial check to be run on him instead of you. He says that he's going to be the co-signer of your loan. Wow! Now there's nothing you can't afford! See, now things have changed: it's not about what you can afford, but about what you desire. If you want a penthouse downtown, the agent will take you to look at it. If you want to see a cottage overlooking a quiet lake, the agent will now take you to it. It's all about desire, for Christ has now qualified you.

This is why in Mark 11:24 the Word of God says, "whatever things you desire when you pray . . . "—it doesn't say, *whatever things you can afford.* And also in John 15:7, Jesus says, "If you abide in Me and My words abide in you, ask what you wish and it shall be given to you." All this is possible because Jesus himself has qualified us for God's blessings. You are born a winner, not a loser. You are now qualified through Jesus' sacrifice, and you do not have to do anything but believe on Jesus and the world is yours. It sounds too good to be true, but it really is true—we just need to believe it.

Stop Pretending and Start Contending

God doesn't like it when a sinner comes to Him and acts like a righteous person, and He doesn't like it when a righteous person comes to Him and acts like a sinner. Remember, faith doesn't work through defeat, it only works through victory. It's like the power of electricity: Electricity doesn't flow through rubber or leather, but flows through copper and steel. The conductor of the power of God is righteousness, and it flows when you are established in the victory of God working in your life. We need to begin acting like who we are and stop believing in the lies of the enemy. You are not defeated; you are on top of your situations if Jesus is your Lord.

In it to Win It

When I came to Jesus, I was "in it to win," not lose. God is looking for people who will win in life. If you're married, you didn't make that commitment because you were expecting to fail at it later; you got in it to win it. You didn't start a career and work hard just to give it up later. You aren't committed to doing what you're doing in order to fail in the end. In the same way, you were saved not just to be in the army of God, but to be one who wins the battles. Whatever it looks like right now for you, keep believing in the Word of God and refuse to let the lie of condemnation take root. You are a winner. Period. Your victory has been sealed in Christ!

Chapter 2
Convinced or Convicted?

Is it a good thing to be convicted of sin in our lives?

Let me answer this question by giving you some personal examples.

As a younger person, I remember going to church and thinking the more forcefully a message was preached, the better it was. But after being in ministry all these years I've learned something: Just because people may feel convicted doesn't guarantee they'll respond to that conviction. In fact, I discovered the harder a message was preached, the less people would actually respond. The Lord, however, showed me how to bring about lasting change within people. It's to preach in a way that establishes them in the area of righteousness.

Hebrews 10:1, 2
"For the law, having a shadow of the good things to come, and not the very image of the things, can never with these same sacrifices, which they offer continually year by year, make those who approach perfect. For then they would not have ceased to be offered? For the worshipers, once purified, would have had no more consciousness of sins."

The very fact that those living under the Old Testament law repeatedly offered sacrifices is the reason they had sin consciousness. If they had offered up a one-time sacrifice, it would have indicated that all of their sins were forgiven for all time. The idea of a one-time sacrifice clearly conveys our sins are forgiven and removed forever. In verse 12 of Hebrews chapter 10 it says that, "But when this priest (Jesus) had offered for all time one sacrifice for sins, he sat down at the right hand of God..." and in verse 14, "For by one sacrifice he has made perfect forever those who are being sanctified."

What does that mean, exactly? If you look again at the verse in context, the writer of Hebrews is showing that in the old covenant a person's sins were only covered; not removed. The fact that they had to return year after year to offer the same sacrifice proves that their sins had never been completely removed from them. The writer of Hebrews makes it clear that if the sacrifices for sin had not been repeated, there would have been no more sin consciousness, or an awareness of sin. We can conclude then, that after we believed on Christ, he through his sacrifice, freed us from sin consciousness. When an individual possesses sin consciousness, they believe they are not completely forgiven. The truth is, we are completely forgiven through Jesus's sacrifice, but sometimes we think like those under the law and develop sin consciousness all over again.

Origin of Sin Consciousness

In the beginning before sin entered the world, there was no sin consciousness in man. In fact, there was neither condemnation nor guilt—none at all. Sin consciousness came after Adam sinned, after he partook of the tree of good and evil. We can then say that sin consciousness, condemnation, guilt, and fear are by-products of sin, just like sickness, disease and poverty are also by-products of sin. Poverty, sickness, and spiritual death did not exist until Adam had sinned. Death came into the world after that event. Before sin came, nothing aged, nothing became corrupt; it was a perfect world.

Romans 5:12
"Therefore just as through one man sin entered the world, and death through sin, and thus death spread to all men because all sinned."

Sin consciousness, condemnation, guilt, and fear clearly stem from sin.

The substance of fear is condemnation; the substance of faith in God is the gift of righteousness. If you find your faith is failing, it could be because you are failing to keep in mind the substance of the gift of righteousness. Whenever we feel condemned it becomes the substance of fear, and that is why it has the ability to affect our prayer life. When we get re-established in the truth of righteousness, we have the substance of faith, and we are then able to freely receive what we need from the Lord. When we begin to doubt our righteous standing with God, it's usually because we switch over to trying to gain righteousness by works instead of believing we are righteous through our faith, paid for by Christ himself.

Once righteousness comes through works, it then has to be maintained by works; this is why faith can go up and down. Praise God our righteousness comes from Jesus dying on the cross. Our righteous standing is firm because it's based on his obedience and not our own. Let me give you an example of this truth. Let's say you were standing on a sandy beach and you were writing your name in the sand. Maybe it looked really beautiful, but once the tide rolled in it wiped your name away. Now let's say you wrote your name in wet concrete. Once it dried, no amount of water could wash it away. We need to become established in our faith so that no matter what life throws at us we'll remain thoroughly convinced of our right standing with God.

How Do You Change?

Many people who desire change in their lives try to make outward changes, but God's grace is what helps people truly change from the inside out, not the outside in.

> *2 Corinthians 3:17, 18*
> *"Now the Lord is the Spirit; and where the Spirit of the Lord is, there is liberty. But we all, with unveiled face, beholding as in a mirror the glory of the Lord, are being transformed into the same image from glory to glory, just as by the Spirit of the Lord."*

These are a very powerful verses. It reveals to us that we change, not by doing but by beholding. The scriptures don't say that we are changed through behavior modification. They don't say we're changed by re-adjusting our habits. The Bible says we are changed by looking at Jesus and believing that as he is, so are we in this world (1 John 4:17). The more we set our mind on things above—where Christ rules—the more we realize we are called to be like him. We must look to Jesus and his righteousness and believe we, too, are righteous. Beholding his holiness and believing we are no longer sinners, but saints—this is what changes us.

Romans 12:2 also shows us that we are transformed from the inside out.

> *Romans 12:2*
> *"And do not be conformed to this world, but be transformed by the renewing of your mind, that you may prove what is that good and acceptable and perfect will of God."*

The word *transformation* implies that change happens from the inside out: it comes through believing (renewing the mind), not "doing."

Now, let's look at another encouraging verse that tells us the truth about who we are in Christ.

> *1 John 3:2*
> *"Beloved, now we are children of God; and it has not yet been revealed what we shall be, but we know that when He is revealed, we shall be like Him, for we shall see Him as He is."*

God is Greater

How do you get rid of guilt, fear, and condemnation in your heart? Let me show you very clearly how to uproot this sin consciousness which produces those feelings that negatively affect your life.

> *1 John 3:20-21*
> *"For if our heart condemns us, God is greater than our heart, and knows all things. Beloved, if our heart does not condemn us, we have confidence toward God."*

When John wrote this letter to encourage the church, it was to remind them of this wonderful truth designed to get their confidence back when it faltered, and that was to remind them that God is "greater than our hearts" and that He knows all things. The text doesn't say to go and do the right thing and once you do, you'll have confidence in God again. No! He simply says God is greater than your heart.

Why does John tell the church that God is "greater than your heart"? This expression that God is greater is also used in the following verse:

John 10:29
"My Father, who has given them to Me, is greater than all; and no one is able to snatch them out of My Father's hand."

Another way of expressing this truth would be to say that God is greater than the actions of men. His power is greater, and He is able to keep those who are His through His own faithfulness, and not depend on our faithfulness. Remind yourself of this powerful truth by also meditating on this verse:

1 John 4:4
"You are of God, little children, and have overcome them, because He who is in you is greater than he who is in the world."

Greater Friend

Let's say you owed one of your friends a great deal of money, and the day had arrived for you to reconcile your debt. You knew you didn't have the funds to pay it back, so you went to your friend asking for more time. You and your friend begin arguing because he wants you to pay it immediately. Now you're upset because you realize it's impossible to ever repay this debt. Suddenly, another friend of yours who loves you very much enters the conversation and says that he'll pay the entire amount you owe. At that moment he throws the money down on the table and tells you it's all taken care of. He's the greater friend, for he had the ability to pay your debt. When the scriptures say God is greater, we understand that it's through Christ's behavior that we can overcome, not through our own behavior which fluctuates and fails at times.

Sin Consciousness Destroys Confidence

I've known born-again believers who were afraid of taking on more responsibilities on the job because they were afraid they'd backslide due to one concern or another (extra stress or excessive travel as examples) and put their family through unnecessary hardships. This sort of thinking can actually be more dangerous because it can hold back people from embracing the right things in their lives. To show you this, let's look at Matthew 25, at the parable of the talents. In this parable, Jesus talks about a man and his three servants. The man leaves his servants in charge of a certain number of talents, each according to the servants' ability. The first servant received five; the second two, and the third received only one. When the man later returned for an account of his money, he saw that the first servant doubled his investment; likewise the second servant. The man was happy with the diligence shown by the first two servants, but he was angered by the third servant who only kept his talent hidden in the ground, not bothering to make an investment. You could say the third servant barely took care of what was left in his care, for he did nothing with it. You can see how the man felt about that last servant. In Matthew 25:28, the man says to give the one talent to the servant who now has ten.

Here's my question regarding this parable: Why give the one talent to the servant who already had ten? Why not give it to the guy that was originally given two? It would seem more fair, right? That servant didn't have as much to begin with, so why not spread it out a little? The reason, I believe, is because Jesus was trying to show us in part that those who understand their responsibility have a greater capacity to help others. When we operate outside of sin consciousness, it allows us the confidence to take on responsibility in a greater way in order to help others more effectively. Think about it in a practical, modern sense: In every major city there are large companies, and if those companies shut down, not only would people be out of work, but the city's overall economy would be affected. Sub-contractors, vendors, even local restaurants would feel the strain, not to mention the economic burden that it would leave on state and local taxes.

My point in all of this is for you to see how the righteousness of God operates. God's righteousness allows us to take on more and receive more out of life. Understanding this truth will give you more confidence in your prayer life, and it will remove man-made limits you may have placed on yourself.

Sin Consciousness is Evil

Have you ever known someone who was deliberately sinning, and you were praying that person would come under heavy conviction so they they'd repent of their sin? If that person only feels convicted, they won't change. Whenever someone's conscience is convicting them of sin, it's an evil conscience. Whenever someone has a conscience of righteousness, they have a good conscience. I know this may sound unconventional, but hear me out, and you'll see where I'm going with this.

Hebrews 10:19-23
"Therefore, brethren, having boldness to enter the Holiest by the blood of Jesus, by a new and living way which He consecrated for us, through the veil, that is, His flesh, and having a High Priest over the house of God, let us draw near with a true heart in full assurance of faith, having our hearts sprinkled from an evil conscience and our bodies washed with pure water. Let us hold fast the confession of our hope without wavering, for He who promised is faithful."

Note the use of the term, "having our hearts sprinkled from an evil conscience." This verse shows us that through an awareness of our true identity which was given to us through the blood of Jesus, we are to boldly come before him. We can only do this when we see ourselves in right standing with God. Operating under an evil conscience creates a need to justify or excuse whatever it is that keeps us under conviction.

This is why Paul said to "awake to righteousness and sin not" (1 Corinthians 15:34). He didn't say, 'awake to sin consciousness and sin not.' Why did he say that? Because righteousness is the foundation of faith. When you have faith, it's rooted in the gift of righteousness, and when you operate by that awareness of righteousness, your faith will be strong enough to enable you to overcome any obstacles in your life.

Now let's look at another scripture that sheds light on this truth. In his first letter to the Corinthians, Paul had to correct some behavior that was going on in the church. He had been informed that there were members of the church who were having sex with prostitutes. But before he even addresses the issue, we find this:

1 Corinthians 6:12
"All things are lawful for me, but all things are not helpful. All things are lawful for me, but I will not be brought under the power of any."

Why in the world would he write such a thing? I believe Paul did it for one reason: He didn't want to stir up a sin consciousness, but rather desired to stir up a righteous conscious within them. In order to be established in righteousness, we must be reminded that we're not under the law, and when we are not under the law, we don't need to worry about the law. That statement may seem almost arrogant, but here's an example that will help clarify what I mean. If you're in Germany driving on the Autobahn, you don't have to necessarily concern yourself with getting a ticket for driving fast, but if you're driving fast, it's possible you could end up in a car crash and kill yourself. It's not the law you have to be concerned with, but about reckless behavior that could warrant some other consequence.

In getting back to Paul, right after he tells them that all things are lawful but not helpful, he continues with the following in his letter:

1 Corinthians 6:15-20
"Do you not know that your bodies are the members of Christ? Shall I then take the members of Christ and make them members of a harlot? Certainly not! Or do you not know that he who is joined to a harlot is one body with her? For 'the two,' He says, 'shall become one flesh.' But he who is joined to the Lord is one spirit with Him. Flee sexual immorality. Every sin that a man does is outside the body, but he who commits sexual immorality sins against his own body. Or do you not know that your body is the temple of the Holy Spirit who is in you, whom you have from God, and you are not your own? For you were bought at a price; therefore glorify God in your body and in your spirit, which are God's."

Paul doesn't try to change them with behavior modification techniques; he gives them the keys to lasting change by teaching and establishing them in the way of righteousness.

Whenever you're convicted of sin in your life, what you do next is very important. If you continue to be convicted by that consciousness of sin, you'll internalize that and end up going further down that road of sin. This is why Paul states in Romans 5:20 that sin increased after the law had been given. That sin consciousness created the need to justify and excuse behavior.

I could never understand how I could preach on something one week, like telling the people about the dangers of compromise, but by the next Sunday they'd act as if they'd never heard the message. Sometimes I'd say to myself, *They just won't change*, but the problem wasn't the people; it was me. I was not teaching in a way that would establish them in righteousness. If I had, they would have responded like righteous people rather than unrighteous people.

I was in service once where a preacher was speaking on financial giving. He had all the tithers stand up, hoping to shame the others into tithing. Needless to say, it didn't change anything. On another occasion a pastor friend of mine had a guest speaker come to his church; a speaker who was really good at teaching on giving, and the giving in the church went up about 80%. Was one group more obedient than the other? No. What made the difference was how the truth was presented. If guilt and shame are used to make a point, positive results won't last because it's a method used in the law. If righteousness is taught, it awakens a confidence that is established in grace.

Remember, the law produces a sin consciousness which produces more sin in people's lives. Look at what Romans 7:7,8 says about this:

Romans 7:7,8
"What shall we say then? Is the law sin? Certainly not! On the contrary, I would not have known sin except through the law. For I would not have known covetousness unless the law had said, 'You shall not covet.' But sin, taking opportunity by the commandment, produced in me all manner of evil desire. For apart from the law sin was dead."

We can say it this way as well: *the law awakened sin within me, which also awakened sin consciousness. Once that happened, it took the opportunity to produce more sin within me.* Note in the above verse the last line: "For apart from the law sin was dead." In other words, the power of sin could not have been unleashed until this sin consciousness had first been awakened. Once we believed on Jesus, the gift of righteousness was given to us through faith, and from that point on we have the power to overcome sin in our lives.

First Response

The first thing you must do when you feel convicted or condemned is to remind yourself of your righteous standing that comes from Jesus.

2 Corinthians 5:21
"For He made Him who knew no sin to be sin for us, that we might become the righteousness of God in Him."

What is the first thing that Jesus did to the woman who was caught in the act of adultery? After he had said to the crowd, "He who is without sin cast the first stone," he said to her, "Woman, where are your accusers? Has no one condemned you?" To which she answered, "No one, Lord." Jesus then said to her, "Neither do I condemn you; go, and sin no more." It's important to see that the first point he made was that he himself did not condemn her. He didn't start by telling her not to sin; that was the last thing he said to her. If we don't start in the proper order, we won't have the power to stop sinning.

> **"Condemnation, guilt and fear are by-products that come from sin. Why then would we want to employ methods that use things that stem from evil to try and change to become more like Jesus?"**

Think of the act of holding your breath. The moment you realize you're out of air, you immediately desire to take a fresh breath. It's an immediate physical response for the body to get the oxygen it needs. In a similar way, as soon as you feel condemned, take a breath of the righteousness of God, and then go and do the right thing. This should be the spirit's immediate response to receive what it needs as well: the affirmation of right-standing with God based on Jesus' sacrifice.

Get re-established in the gift Jesus gave you—freedom from condemnation—and then out of that position of right-standing, do what is right. If you try to correct your behavior through the position of "a sinner," then you will continue to sin. But if you begin to examine your behavior from the position of one who is righteous through Christ, you will continue to do the right things.

Deep-Seated Condemnation

When I have weeds in my yard, I put fertilizer on it and it kills most of the weeds. Sometimes, though, the regular dose isn't enough to destroy all of them, so I put a higher dose on those stubborn ones in order to kill those that remain. Like those weeds, I'd like to go just a little deeper here so we can uproot any of those hard places where condemnation may still have a hold in your life.

James 1:17
"Every good gift and every perfect gift is from above, and comes down from the Father of lights, with whom there is no variation or shadow of turning."

Let me ask you, is condemnation a perfect gift? Is guilt a perfect gift? How about fear; is that a perfect gift? Of course not. I want you to remember God did not create condemnation, guilt, and fear. Condemnation, guilt and fear are by-products that come from sin. Why then would we want to employ methods that use things that stem from evil to try and change to become more like Jesus?

Condemnation Kills

When we operate under a spirit of condemnation, it's easy to look at the past and live with regret. We replay mistakes in our minds and our thoughts become full of, *If I hadn't done this*, or *If only I had reacted differently*, or a number of other depressing things. The accuser of the brethren—the devil himself—uses these unfortunate opportunities to keep individuals on that path of condemnation, guilt, and fear, for he is fully aware that this path leads to more mistakes. This is the road that leads to depression, oppression, and sometimes even suicide for the one who can't see a way off this path. If you were driving your car down a street and a sign caught your eye that said WRONG WAY, you'd immediately turn your car around because you know that if you continue in that direction something dangerous could happen; you could even lose your life. Spiritually speaking, whenever you find yourself full of either condemnation, fear, or guilt, you are heading down the wrong path and it's a direction that leads to loss. It is not the road for the believer in Christ. God has a new highway he wants us to drive on, and there is no condemnation, guilt, or fear on it. It is the highway of heaven.

The Holy Spirit

If you're beginning to grasp what I'm teaching you, then what I'm about to say may just terrify you a little bit. I think many people have accepted and embraced the idea that feelings of guilt and condemnation come from the Holy Spirit. Do you realize that in order to believe this, one must believe that the Holy Spirit is using a by-product of evil in order to train believers in righteousness? That's like taking a criminal and employing him to teach us to be good, upstanding citizens. Many of us have been taught that the Holy Spirit will make you feel bad for all your sins; that he will convict you of your unrighteousness, and make you fearful concerning the judgment to come.

> *John 16:8-11*
> *"And when He has come, He will convict the world of sin, and of righteousness, and of judgment: of sin, because they do not believe in Me; of righteousness, because I go to My Father and you see Me no more; of judgment, because the ruler of this world is judged."*

Look carefully at the above passage. The word "sin" is singular. The sin in this text is regarding the sin of not believing in Jesus. The primary purpose of the Holy Spirit is to convict the world of the need for a Savior. Another word for convict is "convince." It is the Holy Spirit's job to convince people that Jesus is the Savior of the world. His secondary purpose, according to these verses, is to reveal that we are righteous through the Savior, and thirdly, that the god of this world (Satan) has been judged and cast out and that we have authority over him.

Do you see that the work of the Spirit is to convince us that we have righteousness through Christ, and to believe that we have authority and dominion over Satan? Another encouraging passage to remember is this:

> *Romans 6:12-14*
> *"Therefore do not let sin reign in your mortal body, that you should obey it in its lusts. And do not present your members as instruments of unrighteousness to sin, but present yourselves to God as being alive from the dead, and your members as instruments of righteousness to God. For sin shall not have dominion over you, for you are not under law but under grace."*

The word "present" here in this text means to *set up, to make ready, to assist or help*. Do not help condemnation, guilt, or fear and do not assist them in getting a foothold into your life! Another interesting word in this verse is the word "instruments." It is the Greek word *hoplon*, which means *tool* or *weapon*. Some Bible translations use the word weapon here. I like that because it shows that condemnation is a weapon of the enemy. Do not give it any place in your life or it might sink your ship!

Paul concludes that sin will not have dominion over you because you are not under the law. Why? Because the law produces condemnation, guilt, and fear.

I grew up with preaching that basically said, *If you're sinning, you need to get right with God*. What was being taught was that if you made some positive changes, you'd have access to God. The message communicated was that your behavior determined your position with Him. This is completely untrue. Nothing you do, whether good nor bad, gives you access to God. What gives you access to God is the gift of righteousness you received when you believed on Jesus Christ.

The entire concept of acceptance through behavior is built on a faulty foundation, driven by performance and works. Righteousness comes from faith. You cannot add to righteousness and you cannot take away from it once Jesus has made you righteous. If I try to "add" to my righteousness, then I'm somehow able to make myself more righteous than someone else. The truth is, whether you've got your life all together or not, if you've believed on Christ, then you and I both stand at the same level of righteousness which is perfect. Now let's examine a verse which I think will get you really excited.

> *Romans 5:1, 2*
> *"Therefore, having been justified by faith, we have peace with God through our Lord Jesus Christ, through whom also we have access by faith into this grace in which we stand, and rejoice in hope of the glory of God."*

The word used for "access" is a word which paints the picture of someone who has gained access to a king, further depicting that at any time, day or night, access is granted. The word "have" is used in the perfect tense, and "stand" is also in the perfect tense. It is a tense which communicates a one-time event. This tense is also used when Jesus was on the cross and said, "It is finished." Indicating that never again would Jesus have to go to the cross.

People who do not believe that you have access to God at all times once you're saved are basically saying that it's up to you whether or not you have access to Him. It's a hopeless situation, kind of like this example. Let's say your car broke down and you head to the store to get the part you need. You try to get into the shop, but there's a sign on the door that says, ACCESS DENIED IF YOUR CAR IS BROKEN. The part you need is in the store, but you can't get it unless your car is fine!

If people think access to God is based on performance, then what will ultimately happen is that there will be a time when they can't maintain their performance—which will prevent them from receiving help in a time of need. The truth is that God helps us when we are involved in sin, and he helps us when we are not.

Keep in mind that it was God who established the covenant you have with Him. Read the story in Genesis 15, where God makes the covenant with Abram. Before He made the covenant with him, it says that Abram fell into a deep sleep. The sleep was supernatural, not a natural sleep. The word for "sleep" is the same word used when God put Adam to sleep when he took his rib and made Eve. You might be wondering what is the significance of putting Abram into this supernatural state. God did this because He knew if Abram was the one to make the covenant, Abram would break it; therefore God made it and swore by Himself. In the same chapter, in verse 17 it states that, "...there appeared a smoking oven and a burning torch that passed between those pieces," (the slain animals used in this blood covenant) which describes what Abram saw when God made His promise.

God the Father is Himself that consuming fire; the burning flame which passed through, and it is Jesus who is the light of the world. Now you have to understand that during that time, blood covenants were often made between landowners, especially in royal land grant treaties. This ritual was very typical and served to seal a deal between the parties making the agreement. Those involved in the deal would walk between the shed blood as a sign to say, *May this be done to me if I don't keep my end of the bargain.* But you can see that it was God alone who sealed the deal, without Abram's assistance or commitment. It was God who swore by Himself so that the covenant would be maintained by His own faithfulness and goodness!

You need to remember this truth: If you can't make it, you can't break it. What I mean by this is that since Abram could not make the covenant, he could not break it. Yet God holds the promise together by Himself. If you are a believer in the Lord Jesus Christ, then this is the covenant of which you are also a partaker.

For years I used to preach to people that they needed to "make Jesus the Lord of your life." At that time I never thought about what I was saying; it was just something I heard others say and said it, too. Where does that saying come from? It comes from the idea that you need to do something before he can rule as Lord over your life. In the first sermon Peter preached (Acts 2:36), he said, "...know assuredly that God had made this Jesus, whom you crucified both Lord and Christ." I can't do anything to make him Lord, but I can believe he is Lord. I don't have the power to put him in that position, but God the Father has already positioned Jesus as Lord.

Some people have deeply rooted condemnation that have been in place for a long time, and this really has the ability to rob from their future. Let me explain. Some people have been divorced several times; others have had abortions; there are those who've hurt loved ones in terrible ways, and sometime after all this, the person involved has a difficult time forgiving himself. If you do not forgive yourself, the full benefits of God's forgiveness cannot flow in your life, and this can greatly affect your future! Think of it: Your entire future outlook, decision-making, even relationships can all be negatively affected through your own self-perception if it's seated in condemnation.

Now, let me show you some verses that have been misinterpreted and used to justify the idea that God would not accept someone because of his sin and thus remove the blessing from him. It's found in Hebrews chapter 12.

Hebrews 12:15-17
"...looking carefully lest anyone fall short of the grace of God; lest any root of bitterness springing up cause trouble, and by this many become defiled; lest there be any fornicator or profane person like Esau, who

for one morsel of food sold his birthright. For you know that afterward, when he wanted to inherit the blessing, he was rejected, for he found no place for repentance, though he sought it diligently with tears."

The reason I say we've looked at this verse incorrectly is because we've gotten the idea that God would not accept Esau because of his sin, but actually the verses are talking about Esau falling short of God's grace. The writer of Hebrews uses the illustration of Esau who sold his birthright and then felt so badly about it he could not forgive himself, which therefore allowed a root of bitterness to grow within him. This is what caused him to be an ungodly man. See, whenever there's an underlying stream of condemnation in your life, it will cause you to live under the dominion of sin. In Esau's case, if he would have forgiven himself, he could have found the heart to repent. If you look at the previous verses carefully, it doesn't say that God rejected him; it says he was rejected for he found no place of repentance. Even though he may have wanted to live differently, he couldn't because of this root of bitterness in his life which grew out of condemnation. If only Esau would have forgiven himself, I believe his story would have turned out much better.

Confession of Sin

In most traditional American churches today, confessing sins is promoted in the church. The idea is that you do not want to have any unconfessed sin in your life, especially if you were to die, so every morning or evening you need to confess your sins. In fact, some people pray in this way: *Lord, please forgive me of these sins . . .* and from there mention each one that comes to memory. Then, to cover all the bases, they may say something like, *Please forgive any other sins I may have committed or have forgotten.* The problem with this approach is that it develops that sin consciousness that we've covered earlier in this chapter. Remember, it's that sin consciousness that stirs up the sin nature. Instead of keeping people from sin, it strengthens sin. We must develop a righteousness consciousness which drives out sin.

Earlier in the chapter, we briefly discussed this next verse, but it bears repeating because it's so important to get this in your heart. 1 Corinthians 15:34 says, "Awake to righteousness and do not sin; for some do not have the knowledge of God. I speak this to your shame." Paul here does not say, *Awake to your sinfulness.* He says to awake to righteousness and do not sin. Think again of the woman who was caught in the act of adultery and Jesus saying to her, "I do not condemn you. Go and sin no more." The gift of righteousness is given to us so that we can do just as Jesus said.

Let's look at another set of verses that have often been misunderstood, and therefore, misused.

1 John 1:5-10
"This is the message which we have heard from Him and declare to you, that God is light and in Him is no darkness at all. If we say that we have fellowship with Him, and walk in darkness, we lie and do not practice the truth. But if we walk in the light as He is in the light, we have fellowship with one another, and the blood of Jesus Christ His Son cleanses us from all sin. If we say that we have no sin, we deceive ourselves, and the truth is not in us. If we confess our sins, He is faithful and just to forgive us our sins and to cleanse us from all unrighteousness. If we say that we have not sinned, we make Him a liar, and His word is not in us."

For years I was taught that if I, as a believer, walk in darkness, I am breaking fellowship with God and the only way I can restore that fellowship is by confessing my sins (according to 1 John 1:9). What I had been taught was that "walking in darkness" was a term used for sinning as a believer and causing the break in fellowship with God. But let's examine these verses a little more closely. Let's take verse 6 to start. "If we say that we have fellowship with Him and walk in darkness, we lie and do not practice the truth."

As I was meditating on this, the Lord opened this verse up to me by illuminating the expression "walking in darkness." He prompted me to look at how John used that same expression in Chapter 2, verse 9. The verse there says, "He who says he is in the light and hates his brother is in darkness until now." So, according to this verse, "walking in darkness" is likened to hating your brother. I then went over to chapter 3:13-15, where the scriptures say, "Do not marvel, my brethren, if the world hates you. We know that we have passed from death to life, because we love the brethren. He who does not love his brother abides in death. Whoever hates his brother is a murderer and you know that no murderer has eternal life abiding in him."

Suddenly, I realized this truth: The person who walks in darkness is not saved. They are not born again. They do not know God. Therefore, verse 6 is describing someone who proclaims they are saved but is not really saved at all. This verse is not talking about believers, but John is showing the true believer in the church what it truly means to be saved. This is also why in 1 John 2:19 he writes, "They went out from us, but they were not of us; for if they had been of us, they would have continued with us; but they went out that they might be made manifest, that none of them were of us."

It's clear from these verses that John is saying that people who are truly born again are not going to leave the church; that the seed of Christ inside of them is what keeps them. What a powerful truth!

Let's look at these same verses again, but now from this different perspective and see just how wonderful God's promises are for the believer.

> *1 John 1:5*
> *"This is the message which we have heard from Him and declare to you that God is light and in Him is no darkness at all."*

In other words, when you believed in Christ, you were placed in him and in him is no darkness at all. How can that be? Only by every one of our sins being forgiven in our lives, whether past, present, or future.

> *1 John 1:6*
> *"If we say that we have fellowship with Him, and walk in darkness, we lie and do not practice the truth."*

So if we say we have fellowship with Him and walk in darkness (like someone who is not saved), we are lying and the truth is not in us, nor is it being practiced.

> *1 John 1:7*
> *"But if we walk in the light as He is in the light, we have fellowship with one another, and the blood of Jesus Christ His Son cleanses us from all sin."*

This should be the best news you've ever heard! There are many who say the only way you can be cleansed of your sins is if you stop sinning and walk in fellowship. But let me ask you a question. If you're not sinning, then why do you need to be cleansed from all sin? The only time you need to be cleansed from sin is if you are sinning, so the idea that walking in fellowship equates to being sin free is erroneous. There's no reason to be cleansed of sin if there isn't any sin to clean. Let me reiterate this point by simply saying that there's no reason to take a bath if you aren't dirty.

Walking in the Light

What does it mean to walk in the light as He is in the light? 1 John 1:7 doesn't say to walk *according to* the light, but to *walk in* the light. There is a very important distinction between the two. To walk in the light means to walk in the truth of what Jesus has done for us. To walk in the light of the scripture that states, "as he is so are you in this world" means that you have grasped the truth of this scripture and you see your identity is lined up with who Christ is. To walk in the light of the scripture that says, "there is no fear in love; but perfect love casts out fear" means that you are putting this scripture to use in your life and you are recognizing fear for what it is. Walking in the light as He is in the light gives us the ability to pray with confidence because we keep His commandments and do those things pleasing in His sight.

> *1 John 3:21-23*
> *"Beloved, if our heart does not condemn us, we have confidence toward God. And whatever we ask we receive from Him, because we keep His commandments and do those things that are pleasing in His sight. And this is His commandment: That we should believe on the name of His Son Jesus Christ and love one another, as He gave us commandment."*

As we pray we can have confidence toward God as we keep His commandment. In the previous verses we see that the commandment is to believe on Jesus Christ and to love one another. The emphasis is not in "doing," but believing. The phrase "keep His commandments" actually means *to watch over.* In other words, watch over what you believe so that you will show forth fruit from your salvation.

As born again believers, we are walking in the light as Christ is in the light, and his blood is cleansing us from sin day in, day out, at all times. The cleansing power of Jesus' blood is like this: Imagine a little boy who found a nice stone and hid it in the mud so the next day he could play with it. When he retrieved it, the stone was dirty of course, so he took that stone, waded into a creek and placed that stone under a running waterfall. The water continued running over and over it, although the stone was already as clean as could be. Jesus' blood is like that waterfall. Jesus took us and put us under streams of living water and that living water continually washes away the sin in our lives.

Let's return to our examination of 1 John 1:5-10, looking now at the eighth verse.

> *1 John 1:8*
> *"If we say that we have no sin we deceive ourselves, and the truth is not in us."*

Here in this verse, John is talking about false brethren, who, at the time were the Gnostics. The Gnostics believed there was no such thing as sin, and here John is addressing this point, saying that if you say there is no sin, you deceive yourself; in other words, you are not saved.

> *1 John 1:9*
> *"If we confess our sins, He is faithful and just to forgive us our sins and to cleanse us from all unrighteousness."*

Note that the word "sins" used here is not a verb, it's a noun. The scripture does not say we need to confess the action of sin, rather it is about the acknowledgment of sin. You see, a person cannot be saved if they don't believe they need saving. If there is no such thing as sin there's no need for a savior. This thinking is exactly what John was dealing with in the church. There were those who didn't believe there was such a thing as sin, and John had to clearly teach the reality of sin in order to put those in a position where they could be saved.

Let me make something perfectly clear at this time. I am not at all opposed to people telling God they're sorry for what they did or simply admitting, *I blew it, Lord.* In the Bible the only time you see the confession of sins used is when it is in connection to being restored to a brother or sister in the Lord (James 5:16). We also find confession of sin after salvation as testimony (Acts 19:18,19).

All this comes down to the truth that we are not forgiven by works; we are forgiven by believing on Christ Jesus.

For years I was raised in church where I would go to confession and confess my sins and then penance was administered. I was taught that if I carried out my penance then I'd go to heaven as long as I didn't die with mortal sin. According to this teaching, mortal sins are the ones that send you to hell if not confessed, but venial sins are sins you could commit, but still get into heaven. This is a system of works. You do a little penance and you're forgiven (until the next confession). But scripturally, Jesus did not ask me to do anything but to believe on him. When I was saved, he forgave me freely without the act of doing penance.

In scripture, the only sin which is not forgiven is resisting the Holy Spirit, or we could say it is the refusal to believe on Jesus Christ for your salvation.

> *Revelation 20:11-15*
> *"Then I saw a great white throne and Him who sat on it, from whose face the earth and the heaven fled away. And there was found no place for them. And I saw the dead, small and great, standing before God, and books were opened. And another book was opened, which is the Book of Life. And the dead were judged according to their works, by the things which were written in the books. The sea gave up the dead who were in it, and Death and Hades delivered up the dead who were in them. And they were judged, each one according to his works. Then Death and Hades were cast into the lake of fire. This is the second death. And anyone not found written in the Book of Life was cast into the lake of fire."*

I want you to see here that nobody went to hell because of adultery or stealing. No one went to hell because of immoral behavior. The people who went to hell (or to the lake of fire) were people whose names were not found written in the Book of Life. It was the sin of rejecting Christ as their Savior that sent them there. The only mortal sin I can see in scripture, if I use that term, is the sin of rejecting Jesus as Savior. Consider the thief on the cross (Luke 23:39-43) who hung alongside Jesus. He didn't have a chance to do anything to make amends for his wrongdoing; he could only put his trust in the Lord. He couldn't go to church or raise his hand and walk down the altar to get saved. He was saved purely by his act of believing.

Free Indeed

No wonder Jesus said, "Therefore if the Son makes you free, you are free indeed" (John 8:36). Free from what? Free from condemnation and guilt that comes from the belief that one cannot be forgiven. I am so glad I am forgiven and that forgiveness is continually cleansing me of all sin which occurs in my life. It is such a wonderful feeling to know that according to 1 John 4:17, as he is, so am I in this world! This is a promise to any and all who would choose to trust in Christ the Savior.

Chapter 3
Grace is Greater Than Sin

I believe we need to stop underestimating the grace of God which the Lord poured out on the church. As long as you think evil is more powerful and more effective than God's grace, it is going to be difficult—if not impossible—to rise above storms you may be facing in your own life.

I want to share with you why many people never seem to be able to rise above the power of their circumstances or to remove the mountains in their lives. I also want to show you that if you really do not believe God's grace is greater than sin, then that belief will limit how much God can use you. Let's look at a verse that begins to help us understand this.

> *Romans 5:20*
> *"Moreover the law entered that the offense might abound. But where sin abounded, grace abounded much more."*

This verse in scripture clearly tells us that grace produces much more fruit than sin will ever produce. It's true that the law stirred up sin within people and produced evil, but despite that, grace still abounded much more. If you are saying *Amen* to this, then why is it that many people believe evil excels more than grace, or that more people are going to go to hell rather than go to heaven? This debate needs to be settled. I believe the grace of God is greater than sin which is in this world, and scriptures support that view. Let's now look at a passage that has caused a lot of controversy regarding this concept.

Matthew 7:13-14
"Enter by the narrow gate; for wide is the gate and broad is the way that leads to destruction, and there are many who go in by it. Because narrow is the gate and difficult is the way which leads to life, and there are few who find it."

Several years ago, I was mediating on these verses and I was struggling with them, saying to myself, *Does this mean that only a few people will be saved when you consider all the individuals who have ever died? Does this mean there are only a few who inherit the kingdom of God?* I had a hard time with this because of what was stated in Romans 5:20.

If only a few people are going to be saved in comparison to the number of people who have ever lived, then you must conclude that the work of the devil—which has produced sin in this world—has produced greater results than grace. I do not believe sin produces more results than God's grace. I believe the grace of God has accomplished much more than the sin in this world. God is greater than evil; evil is not greater than God.

Let me prove this to you from the Word of God. When God called Abram, He told him that his descendants would be as numerous as the sands of sea and as the stars of the sky (Genesis 15:5). If you tried to count the stars in just one galaxy, the number would be beyond what your mind could comprehend! Now consider that magnitude as you read what is written in Revelation concerning the number of people that will be in heaven.

Revelation 7:9
"After these things I looked, and behold, a great multitude which no one could number, of all nations, tribes, peoples, and tongues, standing before the throne and before the Lamb, clothed with white robes, with palm branches in their hands . . . "

This scripture states there were so many people in heaven it was impossible to count them. I believe if you went to heaven today you would find the housing market has been booming ever since Jesus was resurrected. Think for a moment of all the babies who die from abortion, or children who perish before they reach the age of accountability. Consider the story in the Old Testament in which God told those 20 years and older that they wouldn't enter the promised land for their unbelief (Numbers 14:26-31). If God did not hold those younger ones responsible for their fathers' sin which kept that generation out of the promised land at that time, wouldn't it be justified to say that God would also not hold children accountable who hadn't yet come to the age of accountability in the generations afterward?

Romans 7:9 states, "I was alive once without the law, but when the commandment came, sin revived and I died." This indicates that at one time throughout our lives, namely childhood, God did not hold us accountable to sin. We could make an argument then, that somewhere between the ages of 13 to 20 that God begins to hold individuals spiritually responsible to right and wrong.

Consider all of the young people who have died before they had an opportunity to reach the age of accountability. Think also on the mentally ill, and those who are unable to reason. Now, I'm not trying to start a debate on how God sees children or the disabled. All I know is that God is just and loving, and desires that not one person would be cast into hell.

If what I'm saying is true, then why do you suppose that Jesus said the way which leads to life is narrow? First of all, He was speaking directly to the Jewish people who were under the law at that time. Clearly, the free gift of salvation is difficult for people to grasp when they are trying to achieve salvation through their own works. Unfortunately, self-righteousness has been putting people in hell for thousands of years. It seems when you consider people who have experienced true transformation in their lives, you find that many of these people had to come to "the end of themselves," to a place where they realize their own works will never be good enough to earn their way to heaven.

Broad is the Way of Self-Effort

The entire world in which we live is based on some sort of merit system: if you do well in school, you graduate; if you go to college and earn a degree, then that degree determines what jobs you're qualified to do. If after that, you land a job and perform well, you get promoted, and on and on it goes. Our whole society is built around this concept, which therefore makes it very difficult for most of us to believe in the value of a system which is not performance driven. The gospel of grace runs completely contrary to the world's system; it is not about self-effort, but about belief in what Jesus accomplished for all mankind on the cross.

Colossians 2:13-15
"And you, being dead in your trespasses and the uncircumcision of your flesh, He has made alive together with Him, having forgiven you all trespasses, having wiped out the handwriting of requirements that was against us, which was contrary to us. And He has taken it out of the way, having nailed it to the cross. Having disarmed principalities and powers, He made a public spectacle of them, triumphing over them in it."

If you examine the New King James Version cross-reference, you would find that "the handwriting of requirements that was against us" is actually defined as "a certificate of debt." This definition pertains to the law, for when man broke the law of God they became indebted to it. This is so powerful, for the Lord knew we could never live up to its standards, so he sent His beloved Son Jesus to do it for us.

Now let's look at this next passage in its proper setting. Here, Jesus is dealing with religious leaders who have lowered the standards of the law in order to boast that they had obeyed the law in its entirety. In context, Jesus was dealing with those who were giving a faulty interpretation of the law.

Matthew 5:17-19
"Do not think that I came to destroy the Law or the Prophets. I did not come to destroy but to fulfil. For assuredly, I say to you, till heaven and earth pass away, one jot or one tittle will by no means pass from the law till all is fulfilled. Whoever therefore breaks one of the least of these commandments, and teaches men so, shall be called least in the kingdom of heaven; but whoever does and teaches them, he shall be called great in the kingdom of heaven."

Every "jot" and "tittle" refers to every facet of the law; the moral, civil, and sacrificial part of it have all been fulfilled by Jesus. When Jesus proclaimed that the person who breaks the least of the commandments and teaches others would be least in the kingdom of heaven, he was referring to the religious leaders. As Jesus said, he never came to destroy the law, but came to fulfill it for us. This means that we are able to receive all the benefits of obedience based on his complete and perfect work.

The Law is Like a Mirror

The law never lifted a hand to help people do what was prescribed in it—it is simply a mirror. It reveals everything wrong with you, me, and all of humanity, but Jesus became the end of the law by fulfilling all righteousness. Now, he places his word in our hearts, and as we listen to our hearts and obey him, he lifts the finger of God and enables us to accomplish whatever he has placed within us to do.

Romans 10:4-8
"For Christ is the end of the law for righteousness to everyone who believes. For Moses writes about the righteousness which is of the law, That the man who does those things shall live by them. But the righteousness of faith speaks in this way, Do not say in your heart, 'Who will ascend into heaven?' (that is, to bring Christ down from above) or, 'Who will descend into the abyss?' (that is, to bring Christ up from the dead). But what does it say? 'The word is near you, in your mouth and in your heart' (that is, the word of faith which we preach) . . ."

> "Because God had decided to make a way through Jesus, every single person who would put their trust in him can receive his grace."

Christ's ministry was the end of the law. He fulfilled all the requirements of it and paid the price for breaking it as well. Therefore, when we believe on Christ, we receive all the benefits of obeying the law, not by what we do, but by the One in whom we believe. This is why Paul says in Romans, "...do not say who will ascend . . . " in other words, no one must go to heaven and bring Jesus down and no one needs to go to the grave and bring Jesus back up. Jesus has done it all for us.

How can a drug addict be saved? A prostitute? Someone who has made mistake after mistake in life? Because God had decided to make a way through Jesus, every single person who would put their trust in him can receive his grace. Do you see why grace truly abounds much more over sin?

Romans 4:16
"Therefore it is of faith that it might be according to grace, so that the promise might be sure to all the seed, not only to those who are of the law, but also to those who are of the faith of Abraham, who is the father of us all . . . "

The scripture says that the promise could only be "sure" (firm, stable) if it is of faith. If the promise were dependent on works, it could not be sure for everyone. This is good news for all of us. You can be healed whether you are educated or not; you can overcome addiction whether you are disciplined or not; you can prosper whether you were born in the right part of town or not. The only way it could be sure, firm, and stable is if it totally depended on the work of Christ. If even one part of it was up to us, people could not be delivered because we are too weak, but praise be to God who delivered us from ourselves! The book of Ephesians tells us that in Jesus we are strong.

Ephesians 6:10
"Finally, my brethren, be strong in the Lord and in the power of His might."

Faith Makes You a Winner

Once you have put your trust in Christ, you become a winner. Begin following the example of those who through faith and patience inherit the promises.

Hebrews 6:11, 12
"And we desire that each one of you show the same diligence to the full assurance of hope until the end, that you do not become sluggish, but imitate those who through faith and patience inherit the promises."

I have often wondered why so many in the church follow after people whose faith fails instead of following after people whose faith wins. In the passage above it says we are to follow the example of those who through "faith and patience" inherit the promises. We should be looking for winners in the church and follow their example. What I mean by the term "winner" here is that you should be searching out those whose faith is strong; those who show wisdom and faithfulness; those people who desire to be positive and encouraging, with a real desire and hunger for the things of God. I think that through the years, much of the church has disregarded the winners and find fault with their successes and looked to people who were failing and called their failure success.

Think of it in this way: When it comes to sports, other players learn or improve by imitating those who achieve great success in their field. How come we're not learning from Christians who are winning in life? I believe the devil tries to put our attention on failing in order to keep us from learning how to win. If Satan can get us to think we're on a losing team rather than the winning team, we're going to say things like, *Well, I didn't get healed in this life but I will in the next*, or, *God didn't provide for me in this life, but He will in the life to come.* These are statements that some people buy into which bring defeat into the church.

Once we place our faith in the grace of God, we are going to start winning in life, for Jesus cannot be defeated. We release His victory over our lives when that truth ignites in our hearts. Stop accepting the life of "not enough" and begin to freely receive the life of "more than enough." Stop looking for the smallest portion and start receiving the biggest portion. God has called the church through grace to do great things, and His grace will supply whatever you need—whether it is the grace to obey His word, or to believe in His promises, God will freely provide.

Add to Your Faith

2 Peter 1:2-8
"Grace and peace be multiplied to you in the knowledge of God and of Jesus our Lord, as His divine power has given to us all things that pertain to life and godliness, through the knowledge of Him who called us by glory and virtue, by which have been given to us exceedingly great and precious promises, that through these you may be partakers of the divine nature, having escaped the corruption that is in the world through lust. But also for this very reason, giving all diligence, add to your faith virtue, to virtue knowledge, to knowledge self-control, to self-control perseverance, to perseverance godliness, to godliness brotherly kindness, and to brotherly kindness love. For if these things are yours and abound, you will be neither barren nor unfruitful in the knowledge

of our Lord Jesus Christ." (underline emphasis, added)

The word "add" in this passage is a very important word. It is the Greek word *epichorēgeō* which comes from the root *choregos*. In Athenian drama festivals, a rich individual called the *choregos* would pay great sums of money, and with extravagance, provide for the needs of the drama. Of course, we cannot humanly "add" to the payment Jesus made on the cross for us. But through God's great grace, we are able to add the fruits of salvation to our faith, which gives us a winning spirit. Since God has with great extravagance provided for our faith, we must embrace all He did to make it available to us.

Imagine if you had worked 14 hours a day all your life to leave your children an inheritance and then after you died, they refused to take the money. Or perhaps they took a small amount and only used that. It would appear as though they had not appreciated all your years of hard work to provide for them and their families. This is one of the reasons why I get upset when people refuse to believe for something which God had promised to His children. Some people may say, *Well, those promises aren't for us today,* when the Bible is very clear that all the promises of God are yes and Amen in Christ Jesus. Let's show our gratitude toward his sacrifice and receive everything he died to give us.

Better Promises

It's hard sometimes to get people in the church to believe they can be blessed as much as Israel was in the Old Testament. Remember, they left Egypt with riches, and not one of them was feeble or sick (Exodus 12:33-35; Psalm 105:37), and they occupied the best of the land once they entered their inheritance. But look what Hebrews states:

Hebrews 8:6
"But now He has obtained a more excellent ministry, inasmuch as He is also Mediator of a better covenant, which was established on better promises."

Scripture clearly states our covenant, through Jesus' obedience, is a better covenant with better promises. Let me illustrate with this example. When you buy a new car, it's better than the old one—it has everything the older car had and more. Your old car had four tires, and so does your new car, but the tires on your new car have that "run flat tire" upgrade, so that if you run over a nail, your tire won't even go flat! Your old car had a CD player and manual seats, but now this new car has Sirius XM and those seats are electric and heated. Do you get the point I'm making? The new one has everything and much more.

We have better promises with the new covenant, such as receiving the Holy Spirit. During the times of the old covenant, the Spirit came and then left, but in the new covenant the promise is that He (the Holy Spirit) will remain with us forever. In the old covenant, there was not a promise of eternal life, but the new covenant provided for eternal life.

Hebrews 11:39, 40
"And all these, having obtained a good testimony through faith, did not receive the promise, God having provided something better for us, that they should not be made perfect apart from us."

Those believers who died during the times of the Old Testament had a different promise. Their sins were only covered, and when they died they waited in an upper region of paradise until Jesus was raised from the dead. (I will explain more on this in Chapter 5.) When that happened, the hearts of the just were made perfect and they ascended on high. For the first time the Holy Spirit was given to everyone who believed on Christ and people received the gift of the Holy Spirit. With Jesus Christ, we have truly entered into a better covenant and have been given the best promises.

Chapter 4
The Sin of Adam

How did sin come into the world? Why are people born with a "sin nature"? These are two questions I want to answer for you here in this chapter.

The scriptures tell us that "all have sinned and fall short of the glory of God" (Romans 3:23). That means there is not even one person in all of creation or history who could be good enough to be deserving of heaven. Unfortunately, hell is full of people who thought they might be "good enough."

You may be saying, *Why did God create us this way?* Well, the truth is He did not. The nature we possess right now is the result of another man's sin, the sin of Adam. I wasn't born a sinner because I had committed a sin; I was born a sinner because of the sin of Adam, the reigning head of all mankind. In other words, he represents all men and women; when his seed became corrupt, his offspring became corrupt as well.

Romans 5:12-14
"Therefore, just as through one man sin entered the world, and death

through sin, and thus death spread to all men, because all sinned—(For until the law sin was in the world, but sin is not imputed when there is no law. Nevertheless death reigned from Adam to Moses, even over those who had not sinned according to the likeness of the transgression of Adam, who is a type of Him who was to come."

The purpose of this chapter is to show you that spiritual death did not come through our own sin, but because of Adam's sin. If you look at that last sentence in the scripture above, it says that Adam was a "type of Him who was to come." This is a clear reference to Jesus being like the first Adam, except that Jesus' obedience allowed us to become righteous, and that through Adam's disobedience we were made sinners. That sin nature was passed down to us. Now don't take from this the idea that you and I have not personally sinned. Just like it's a bird's nature to fly, it's man's nature to sin.

You might be in objection here by thinking this isn't fair, or why would God hold others responsible for another's sin? But let's consider the other side of this issue. It isn't "fair" that I should be made righteous by another man, yet I was the day I believed on Jesus. So you see, through the mercy and grace of God, we were given a new representative, a new reigning head of mankind: Jesus, the Savior.

Romans 5:18, 19
"Therefore, as through one man's offense judgment came to all men, resulting in condemnation, even so through one Man's righteous act the free gift came to all men, resulting in justification of life. For as by one man's disobedience many were made sinners, so also by one Man's obedience many will be made righteous."

Let me show you an outstanding truth which will help you become even more established in your righteousness through Christ. We discussed earlier in this book that at the beginning of creation, when Adam and Eve lived and walked with God before sin came into the world, there was no decay, no corruption; there were no disasters of any kind. What do you think happened when Adam and Eve ate fruits from all the trees? Let's say they'd taken a bite out of a fruit and then left that fruit sitting overnight. There would not have been any signs of decay on that fruit at all, because corruption did not yet exist. God made Adam the gatekeeper for this world, so to speak, and sin could not enter it except through him.

This is why in Genesis 3:6,7 we find that their eyes were not opened to this transgression until Adam had eaten the fruit. If Adam had refused to eat it, then Eve never would have died spiritually and sin would have never come into this world.

What is so powerful about this is that Jesus is referred to in scripture as "the last Adam" (1 Corinthians 15:45). Why is he called that? Because during his earthly ministry he was tempted in all areas like the first Adam, but when Jesus was resurrected from the dead, his body was raised in a way in which it cannot be tempted again. Therefore his position is eternal and can never fail.

The only way a born-again believer would lose their salvation or lose the gift of righteousness is if the one who gave it to him sinned, and that cannot happen, praise God. We are able to rest in the finished work of Jesus Christ who accomplished victory over sin once and for all. Once I began to see this in scripture, I rejoiced knowing that it isn't my faithfulness that saves me; that it isn't my goodness that keeps me in the grace of God. It's all through the finished work of Jesus.

If you do a study of Israel coming out of Egypt, you find this same truth in operation. For example, when the Israelites began their exodus, they were completely covered under grace. Psalm 105:37 says with regard to the exodus, "He brought them out with silver and gold, and there was none feeble among His tribes." The Israelites were under such great grace, that not one person had died until the law was given. Once the law was given 3,000 people had died (Exodus 32:28). When the church was born under the gospel of grace, we find the opposite happened: 3,000 people became saved in a day (Acts 2:41). In other words, before the law was given, judgment was based on man's faithfulness and goodness. The people had even told Moses that they would obey and do whatever God said. (Note that it's not a good idea to sign a contract before you read the contents!) This resulted in defeat, for they could not keep the law on their own.

Laws of Interpretation

When studying scripture, there are laws of interpretation that must be heeded in order to understand the word properly. One of these laws is to build understanding from the verses which are clear instead of building from verses which are unclear or ambiguous. If we build from what is clearly communicated first, then we can use that as a foundation for other verses so they can be more easily understood. I want to discuss two sets of verses that people have debated over for 2,000 years.

These scriptures are found in James 2 and Romans 4.

James 2:18-20
"But someone will say, "You have faith, and I have works." Show me your faith without your works, and I will show you my faith by my works. You believe that there is one God. You do well. Even the demons believe—and tremble! But do you want to know, O foolish man, that faith without works is dead?"

Romans 4:4, 5
"Now to him who works, the wages are not counted as grace but as debt. But to him who does not work but believes on Him who justifies the ungodly, his faith is accounted for righteousness,...."

Once you build upon clearer verses regarding this subject, then verses like the one in James make perfect sense. James is talking about the kind of faith which is justified before men; Paul is explaining the kind of faith which is justified before God.

There is no contradiction to be found between these scriptures at all. The explanation found in James shows that when you are authentic in your faith, it will display itself before others. For instance, if you say you love someone you will show it. The scriptures in Romans deals with the act of being saved; that we are justified before God because of what Jesus did.

I have seen many well-meaning teachers within the church body say things like, *I can't take the chance of preaching too heavily on grace. I'm afraid people will stop doing the Word of God.* But if we look at scripture, there's a great stress on what happens if you mix grace and works (trying to merit God's approval through self-effort) together. Paul says in Galatians 1:8 that those who preach a different gospel than the one he taught, those people would be "accursed." I do not find scriptures warning us to be too careful about preaching on grace; in fact, it does just the opposite. The entire book of Galatians is dedicated to ensuring we do not mix works with grace.

Peoples' salvation is at stake when the preaching of grace is taken out of the church. The Bible is quite clear that if people are under works, then they are also under the law.

Being under the law allows sin to dominate, and doesn't allow for the power of God to operate freely. Miracles cannot be manifested in a place where only the message of works is preached.

> *Galatians 3:2-5*
> *"This only I want to learn from you: Did you receive the Spirit by the works of the law, or by the hearing of faith? Are you so foolish? Having begun in the Spirit, are you now being made perfect by the flesh? Have you suffered so many things in vain—if indeed it was in vain? Therefore He who supplies the Spirit to you and works miracles among you, does He do it by the works of the law, or by the hearing of faith?"*

By these scriptures, we can see that turning to our own works instead of trusting in the work of God can be extremely destructive to our faith. Praise God for the wonders of His grace! We are not made righteous from our own obedience, but because of the obedience of His Son, Jesus.

Now you may be asking yourself if it matters whether or not you are obedient or whether or not you try to do well according to God's word. I think many people use the truth about grace to justify actions against obeying the Lord. This is a terrible thing to do to the One who died for us.

Picture this: two people are held hostage in a bank robbery; one is an older man, well along in age, and the other is a young mother of two children. The gunman is prepared to take down one of the hostages, but the older gentleman pleads for the young woman's life and says, "Please, let her live, shoot me instead." The older man thinks about the life ahead of this woman; all of the joy she could receive in raising her children and making a happy home. It would be a great insult to that man's sacrifice if after that, the young mother actually ended up leaving her husband and abandoning her kids so she could go out and party or do whatever else she just felt like doing. In a similar way, Jesus gave his life for us so that we might live a life of fruitfulness and abundance, not so that we would go out and sin.

The scriptures clearly tell us we need to obey the gospel of Christ, according to Romans 1:5, "Through Him we have received grace and apostleship for obedience to the faith among all nations for His name." and Romans 6:17, "But God be thanked that though you were slaves of sin, yet you obeyed from the heart that form of doctrine to which you were delivered."

I have a picture in my house that shows the outstretched arms of Jesus over the cross. The text above reads, *How much does Jesus love you?* And at the bottom it says, *This much.* It should be out of a heart of thankfulness for what he has done and gratitude for the depth of his love that we choose to obey him. It's wrong to misuse the truth regarding our right standing with God based on Jesus' obedience, or to use it as an excuse in order to disobey the Lord, as if his sacrifice didn't matter. When you possess faith, you desire to please God. Disobedience may not have an impact on the truth of your spiritual righteousness in Christ, but it does matter if you want to live a life that is pleasing to the Lord.

Family Forgiveness

There is a form of forgiveness which is different than the kind that is experienced at salvation. If children misbehave within their family, they will go to their parents and tell them they're sorry for what they had done. Most parents will quickly forgive and put the children back in their good graces. But if parents have adult children living outside the home and they break the law, they'd be brought to court on charges whether or not they express to the judge just how sorry they are. The judge in court will treat the children differently because the court system operates in justice to the law, not on mercy. A judge can grant mercy, but it would depend on the offending party's history. In a family, mercy is in operation. In the family of God as well, the Lord gives us mercy, not based our our history, but based on the work of Jesus.

When you know you are forgiven, it's key to forgive others. When you know you are forgiven, it makes it easier to forgive others for the sins they've committed against you. When you become aware of God's riches towards you, it will cause you to be generous towards others. Imagine what kind of person you'd be if someone showed up on your front porch with a check for a hundred million dollars. Let's just say you were chosen to receive this gift and you did nothing to earn it at all. You'd most likely feel so favored that it would cause you to want to help others less fortunate, and your whole world view would change, for you'd constantly be reminded that you didn't deserve this; it just happened. In a similar way this is what happens when Christ comes into our lives, but his rewards are eternally valuable; so much more than money.

Christ has freely given us so much, and when we really grasp this truth it causes us to love others in a way we've been loved by God. If God decided to forgive us before we ever accepted him as Lord, shouldn't we forgive others before they ever decide to apologize for their wrongdoings against us? If God continues to forgive us in our lives, shouldn't we release those things we hold against others? Of course we should. This is why the Bible says we love him because he first loved us (1 John 4:19). The more we walk in the light of truth concerning Jesus, the more we will work out our salvation and the more we will truly experience the power of our salvation.

Whenever we sin after salvation, those sins have already been forgiven, but there is still the need to get right with God so our relationship with Him is healed. It's important to go to Him and admit when we "blow it" because it causes us to humble ourselves. Always remember God's unconditional love for you never changes because you have been forgiven through Jesus' sacrifice.

The more my thinking aligns with God's word, the more God's grace fills my sails and it becomes easier to serve Him. It's not hard to seek the Lord when God's presence is at my back. When I first caught hold of this truth about righteousness, it was difficult for me to accept it. But once I began seeing this truth at work in my life I realized I no longer had to strive in my efforts in order to gain more favor from God. Instead, I began resting in the free gift of righteousness. What a relief, what a peace it brought to my soul! My relationship with Jesus began growing deeper and my walk with God just kept getting stronger and stronger.

I'm alarmed that in America many churches are doing away with the altar. Why? Are we creating a gospel which no longer promotes seeking the face of God? Has the desire to make things convenient and achieve results quickly made us less useful for our King? Has the church in America left its first love? Perhaps we need to remember how far from where we have fallen and begin doing things like we did when we first met Him. We must return to having a desire to just be in His presence. I remember days where I would just spend every moment trying to feel as close to Him as possible. I was so grateful for what Jesus had done for me, that I simply desired to be with Him. When you have a real love for someone, just being in their presence is enough.

These truths I'm bringing out from the Bible were never designed by God to give us an excuse to disobey Him. In fact, the gospel directs us to obey in faith. When we receive this revelation, we understand it's for the purpose of assuring us that whatever mistakes we've made in life that we can still come to the Lord for help. We don't have to go by our own strength and earn the right to get into His presence. Come to Him just as you are, whether you're broken, or weak, or strong, it makes no difference. Grace was given to us so that we would have dominion over sin, and that sin would not prevail over us.

Chapter 5
Is God Mad at Me?

I remember when I first came to the Lord and I was in that "honeymoon phase" with Him. Everything was new and refreshing. It was certainly a wonderful time, but then I hit my first really tough trial. Suddenly, I began to have doubts about myself and about how God was treating me.

There were two basic thoughts which came to my mind at that time. The first one was, *Have I done anything that has caused this present situation?* The second thought was, *Is God punishing me for things I did before I came to Jesus?* What added fuel to that fire in my thinking was a well-meaning believer who would point out weaknesses I had. He had an overall judgmental demeanor when he spoke to me that caused me to feel like I was always doing something wrong. During those early years, I only knew this—that Satan came to steal, kill, and destroy, and that Jesus came to give me abundant life. Even though I couldn't articulate it at the time, I knew deep down in my heart that the problem was related to Satan, not God punishing me. I believe I was spared from a lot of grief because of how the Holy Spirit had led me through that particular period, but so many have grown up in churches that have displayed an inaccurate image of God, stirring up doubts about His goodness.

God is not up in heaven with a big stick just waiting to hit His children over the head when we mess up. His deep love for us was displayed on the cross which removed all wrath toward us. To show you very clearly from God's word, I want to go through some verses in Isaiah chapter 54 which will help us understand how God's wrath was satisfied at the cross. Before we look at those verses, we have to understand the proper context in which those verses were written, which means we must examine the scriptures that come before it. Let us start by looking at some verses of Isaiah 53:

Isaiah 53:3-5
"He was despised, and we did not esteem Him.
Surely He has borne our griefs
And carried our sorrows;
Yet we esteemed Him stricken,
Smitten by God, and afflicted.
But He was wounded for our transgressions,
He was bruised for our iniquities;
The chastisement for our peace was upon Him,
And by His stripes we are healed."

We can clearly see Isaiah 53 points to Jesus. Take special note of the prophecy that states, "He was wounded for our transgressions, He was bruised for our iniquities; the chastisement for our peace was upon Him, and by His stripes we are healed."

Immediately, starting in the next verses, the beginning of chapter 54, Isaiah writes, "Sing, O barren, you who have not borne! Break forth into singing, and cry aloud, you who have not labored with child! For more are the children of the desolate than the children of the married woman," says the Lord." Here Isaiah prophesied that the coming church age would bear more fruit than was ever produced under the law of Moses. He then begins to explain how in that coming church age God would never again be angry with His people.

Isaiah 54:9, 10
"For this is like the waters of Noah to Me;
For as I have sworn
That the waters of Noah would no longer cover the earth,
So have I sworn

That I would not be angry with you, nor rebuke you."

These verses should settle once and forever that the moment you believed on Christ, God would never be angry with you again. What Isaiah is revealing here is that the type of anger displayed during the age of Noah was God's wrath. As it says that, "So have I sworn that I would not be angry with you, nor rebuke you," the term "rebuke" here talks of being rebuked out of His wrath. Psalm 95:11 and Hebrews 3:3 speak of God swearing ". . .in My wrath they shall not enter My rest." This is in reference to the first generation of Israel who refused to mix their faith with the promise of possessing the promised land, and God became so angry with them He swore in His wrath they would die in the wilderness. The good news is this will never happen to the believer, for God poured out his wrath upon His son on the cross for us. All of our sins were placed upon the body of Jesus, so now God deals with us out of mercy and grace.

Jesus has removed all possibility of wrath being poured out on you. There is no reason to believe God is angry with you and punishes you for mistakes from your past. Here is another verse that clearly demonstrates God's position on this subject.

1 Thessalonians 5:9,10
"For God did not appoint us to wrath, but to obtain salvation through our Lord Jesus Christ, who died for us, that whether we wake or sleep, we should live together with Him."

Double Jeopardy

The 5th Amendment of the U.S. Constitution is the Double Jeopardy Clause, which prohibits state and federal governments from prosecuting individuals for the same crime on more than one occasion, or imposing more than one punishment for a single offense. At the cross, Jesus died for all of your sins past, present, and future, which means that God will never bring those sins up against you again. You will never be in danger of Double Jeopardy, spiritually speaking. If the Lord was to try you again for your sins, it would be a miscarriage of justice.

Some of you may be saying, *I can agree that God forgave me of my sins up to the point of salvation, but how can they be forever forgiven after salvation?* To those who would say this, let me ask you: Since Jesus died for you over 2,000 years ago, were not all of your committed sins "in the future"? If his payment did not cover all sin, then how did God choose which ones to forgive on the cross? Another question I would ask you is this: How could God swear that He would never again place His wrath upon you if only some of your sins were forgiven? When you begin to look at this from God's point of view, it's not hard to believe that all of our sins have been forgiven—past, present, and future.

The Israelite's sins however, had to be covered or atoned for time and time again. Let's compare the on-going sacrifices of the Old Testament to Jesus' one-time sacrifice by reading Hebrews 10:11-14.

Hebrews 10:11-14
"And every priest stands ministering daily and offering repeatedly the same sacrifices, which can never take away sins. But this Man, after He had offered one sacrifice for sins forever, sat down at the right hand of God, from that time waiting till His enemies are made His footstool. For by one offering He has perfected forever those who are being sanctified."

The sacrifices performed under the law of Moses served not only as a reminder of the sins people committed; these repeated sacrifices also revealed that the people were never completely cleansed. If an individual was really honest about their sins, sacrifices were also a very expensive investment. If you were rich, you had to take a prize bull and offer it up; if you were a person of little means you had to offer up a lamb. For those who were considered poor, they had to offer smaller animals, but no doubt, it was costly to pay for sins. One of the reasons why the priests began lowering the standards of the law was not to justify sins, but to make it a less expensive obligation for the people. This is ironic when you think of the costly sacrifice Jesus made for us; he gave everything he had and everything he was.

Jesus forgave you for all of your sins, past, present, and future. Some have misinterpreted biblical teachings and therefore have made it difficult to grasp this truth.

To show you what I mean, let me share with you a teaching that is often misinterpreted. Let's take the parable of the ten virgins. Jesus said five were ready for the bridegroom and five were not. When I was younger

I heard preachers who would say that if you are not filled with the Holy Spirit when Jesus returns, you'd be left behind. But if you look at the end of the parable, Jesus makes it clear that the ones who were left behind were the ones he did not know (Matthew 25:12). Keep in mind Jesus said in John 10:27 "My sheep hear My voice, and I know them and they follow Me." Another particular passage which sheds light on those who will be truly left behind is in the seventh chapter of Matthew.

Matthew 7:21-23
"Not everyone who says to Me, 'Lord, Lord,' shall enter the kingdom of heaven, but he who does the will of My Father in heaven. Many will say to Me in that day, 'Lord, Lord, have we not prophesied in Your name, cast out demons in Your name, and done many wonders in Your name?' And then I will declare to them, 'I never knew you; depart from Me, you who practice lawlessness!'"

Years ago, my Greek Studies instructor told me the statement, "I never knew you," literally means *I never knew you at any time in your life.* What these verses tell us then is that there is no one cast into hell who has ever been known by Jesus. If that were not true, then Jesus would have had to say something like, *Depart from me those who I used to know but no longer know.* He does not say, *Well, I used to know you when you were sixteen and you got saved at youth camp, but you fell away later in life.* No! You are either known by Him or not. If you have believed in Jesus, then when he returns for the church you will not be left behind. This does not give license to do these things, but if you are not living right, or if you are sinning at the time God's trumpet blows, you will go up because God will not punish you with His wrath.

Romans 6:1, 2
"What shall we say then? Shall we continue in sin that grace may abound? Certainly not! How shall we who died to sin live any longer in it?"

These verses used to trouble me. Paul was accused of teaching in such a way that allowed people to believe they could continue to sin because of his great emphasis on the grace of Jesus Christ. For years, I was actually ashamed I had never been persecuted for preaching the gospel. However, ever since I began to preach the gospel of grace and stress Christ's work in this way, many people have criticized me by saying that I am giving people license to sin. The truth is that corrupt men will always take the word of truth and twist it for their own means. Those with pure motives will preach on the power of grace and possess a true desire for others to become closer to God and become more like Him.

Perfected Forever

Hebrews 10:14
"For by one offering He has perfected forever those who are being sanctified."

According to this verse, how long are you perfected? Forever. Can you see the impact of this truth in your life? Can you see that through Jesus' one-time sacrifice, it has forever perfected those found in Him? This "new man," this new person is you. I believe as you are grasping the truth of this, there is purity which is just bubbling up in your spirit.

I believe without a doubt Jesus died once and for all for our sins. But I don't believe this means there is a one-time cleansing. 1 John 1:7 says, "But if we walk in the light as He is in the light, we have fellowship with one another, and the blood of Jesus Christ His Son cleanses us from all sin." This makes it clear that the blood of Jesus cleanses us continually in our lives.

It's like going to the beach with your kids: While they're on the shore they get so dirty, but once they decide to get into the water, all the dirt falls off. If they begin to throw wet sand on each other and they become a mess, they jump right back into that water and become clean once again. So it is with Christ. As we believed on him and submerge ourselves in living water, He is washing away the filth in our lives.

Picture a glass of water that has some mud at the bottom. Now picture placing that glass under a running faucet. The water pouring into that glass will wash up that dirt and out of the glass, making it clean once again. Once you are born again, there is a continual flow of purity from Christ that pours into you, washing away sins. It is an on-going process and it never stops; it goes on and on. You do not lose your spiritual life. This is why you remain spiritually alive even when you sin or even when you put things before God.

If this wasn't true, then what assurance would we have that our salvation is eternal? What, if after we've been in heaven for a millenium, you slipped up one day and lost your temper? Does this mean God would cast you out of heaven? Absolutely not, for Jesus' one-time sacrifice perfected us forever. So what exactly is perfected? Our minds are not, and this is why we are to renew our minds to the Word of God so that we may grow in spiritual maturity. What is perfected is the inner man, the real "you," which is continually being purified by the sacrifice of Jesus on a daily basis. Oh, what a wonderful truth!

1 John 3:9
"Whoever has been born of God does not sin, for His seed remains in him; and he cannot sin, because he has been born of God."

Most Bible translations say, "he who has been born of God does not habitually sin. His seed remains in him and he cannot habitually sin because he has been born again." So it is because of the seed of Christ in us that we do not habitually sin or sin like we had before we met Jesus. At that time we were spiritually dead, but now when we sin it is done in the light. We can think of it in this way: Is it possible to stumble over your own feet in the light? Sure, but if you're in the dark, you stumble a lot more because you're unable to see.

If you do a study on the Holy Spirit, you'll discover in the Old Testament that the Holy Spirit usually only came upon prophets, priests, and kings, and the Holy Spirit did not permanently remain upon anyone. The Spirit would fall and then lift; this is why David, after he had sinned, prayed and wrote, "Do not cast me away from Your presence, and do not take Your Holy Spirit from me" (Psalm 51:11). It is only after the resurrection of Jesus that the Holy Spirit could come and dwell with us forever. The Holy Spirit could not do this if there was sin in our spirits, but since Jesus has perfected our inner man through his one-time sacrifice, it is possible to have the Holy Spirit live forever with us. Now, let's look at another scripture that verifies this statement.

John 14:16
"And I will pray the Father, and He will give you another Helper, that He may abide with you forever . . . "

How long? What did Jesus say? Forever. This could never be possible if we had not been perfected in the inner man. In fact, when Jesus rose from the dead, the Bible says, "He lead captivity captive" (Ephesians 4:8). The Old Testament saints who died before Jesus came were kept in the place called paradise. They had yet to be purified by a perfect sacrifice. But after Jesus rose from the dead, those saints were born again, and then for the first time in history, humanity occupied heaven. Captivity had now been made captive by Jesus.

Hebrews 12:22-24
"But you have come to Mount Zion and to the city of the living God, the heavenly Jerusalem, to an innumerable company of angels, to the general assembly and church of the firstborn who are registered in heaven, to God the Judge of all, to the spirits of just men made perfect, to Jesus the Mediator of the new covenant, and to the blood of sprinkling that speaks better things than that of Abel."

It says here that the heavenly Jerusalem is the place of the church of the firstborn. These scriptures speak of those who believed in God before the work of the cross, but after that, those spirit beings were made perfect through the new birth. It is Christ in us who has purified our inner man. It is the precious blood of the Lamb that was shed for you and me and it continues to cleanse us day in and day out throughout our lives.

Please understand this. We should not be working *for* victory, rather we ought to be working *from* that place of victory in our lives! So the position that we stand in is a position of victory and dominion, accomplished for us by Jesus' sacrifice.

If we really desire to become more like Jesus, we must stop looking at all of our faults and instead focus on who we are in Christ. Years ago, when Joyce and I were young parents, our children would help me act like who I really was in Christ. Let me explain. When I would begin acting in an unbecoming way, they would say to me, "*Pastor*, what are you doing?" They didn't say, *Dad!* They would always say, "Pastor!" They were reminding me of my calling. It is the new identity we have in Christ that we need to focus on; the new man in Christ Jesus. Anyone can find fault with oneself and with others, but true spiritual growth happens when you recognize who you are in Christ. As you become aware of your new identity, you start recognizing behavior that doesn't fit the "new man." You begin saying to yourself things like, *This is no way a new man in*

Christ should act. When facing problems, you begin to change old habits and you begin to say things like, *Wait a minute. I have authority over this. I don't need to take anymore of this in Jesus' name.* You begin moving forth in your position of righteousness. I have countless situations in my life where this new man would rise up inside of me and I would take authority over issues and healing would come forth and mountains would be removed.

In Zechariah 4:7 the scripture says, "Who are you, O great mountain? Before Zerubbabel you shall become a plain!" In other words regarding the issue he faced, the word to Zerubbabel from the Lord was, *You are no match for my anointed servant Zerubbabel.* Likewise, you must remember that no problem and no devil is any match for you, the believer, who has been seated in heavenly places in Christ Jesus.

I think the church for a large part, has spiritual amnesia. Most believers have either never been told who they are in Christ, or they had been taught but have forgotten their true spiritual identity.

There's an old story of an eagle who laid her eggs on the side of a cliff. One day, one of the eggs fell out of the nest and landed unharmed on the ground below. A farmer who lived close by saw what had happened but was unable to return the egg back to its place. The farmer took the egg home and put it under one of the hens in the chicken coop. The egg hatched and this little eaglet was raised with the chickens. He spent his days eating worms and digging at the dirt under his feet. One day he looked up and saw this majestic bird soaring in the sky overhead. The growing eaglet thought to himself, *I wish I was like that bird.* Since that eaglet didn't believe he himself was that kind of bird, he just continued to act like the chickens around him. After a while, his wings grew out and one day he again saw that majestic eagle fly overhead. The young eagle began flapping his large wings and instead of just going a few feet like his friends the chickens, he started to climb higher and higher into the sky. His true nature kicked in and he suddenly realized that indeed, he was an eagle.

I believe many people in the church today live like "chickens." Instead of soaring, they look at everything soaring over them. We must realize we were designed for much more in life. Spread your wings and begin to soar! Every time someone reminds you of your past, or how "unqualified" you may be, remind yourself of who you are in Christ, and that it is your destiny to move beyond any barriers you may encounter. Begin rising to those greater heights. It's truth like this which will cause your wings to grow and become strong. The more they grow, the higher you will be able to fly in life.

Chapter 6
Is It Harder Than It Should Be?

Is it possible that when it comes to obeying and following the Lord that it's harder than it should be? Could it be that because of a lack of understanding we make obedience more difficult than it really is? There are many verses which would suggest this is true.

> *Matthew 11:28-30*
> *"Come to Me, all you who labor and are heavy laden, and I will give you rest. Take My yoke upon you and learn from Me, for I am gentle and lowly in heart, and you will find rest for your souls. For My yoke is easy and My burden is light."*

The word "light" in Greek is *elaphros*, which suggests something easy to carry, such as a wallet or a purse.

> *1 John 5:3*
> *"For this is the love of God, that we keep His commandments. And His commandments are not burdensome."*

Within these two verses, we get the sense that God wants us to somehow consider our situations differently than how we may normally perceive them. This may not be how we feel about our problems or burdens, therefore I ask the question: Is it harder than it should be to truly follow Jesus?

I believe one of the reasons why it is difficult for some and easier for others is based on perspective. Like, for example, two guys who need to go to the gym after a long day at work. One guy says he has to go to the gym but doesn't want to do it. He says he's only doing it to get his cholesterol down and besides, if he doesn't work out his wife will give him grief about it when he gets home. The other fellow is really looking forward to heading to the gym. In fact, he's going to pick up his wife so they can work out together before dinner. Both of these men will be working out, but one is doing it out of necessity and the other is doing it out of love and interest. Doing things out of love are always easier than doing things out of necessity. 1 John 4:19 tells us that "we love him because he first loved us." Isn't that amazing? It's easier to work from a heart of love than one of obligation. The more we learn of God's great love for us, the easier it is to sacrifice—or to do seemingly difficult things—for Him.

Years ago when God called me and my wife to go to Bible school, we sold our home and all our belongings in order to be able to go. Many people thought that we had sacrificed a lot to follow the Lord. When people would ask us about our decision we'd both say that it didn't seem like a great sacrifice to us at all. God had done so much for us and we felt honored and blessed to be able to follow Him. Our perspective was one of gratitude, not obligation.

I want to give you three important truths which will lighten the load in your life.

Galatians 3:7-14
"Therefore know that only those who are of faith are sons of Abraham. And the Scripture, foreseeing that God would justify the Gentiles by faith, preached the gospel to Abraham beforehand, saying, "In you all the nations shall be blessed." So then those who are of faith are blessed with believing Abraham. For as many as are of the works of the law are under the curse; for it is written, "Cursed is everyone who does not continue in all things which are written in the book of the law, to do them." But that no one is justified by the law in the sight of God is

evident, for "the just shall live by faith." Yet the law is not of faith, but "the man who does them shall live by them."

Christ has redeemed us from the curse of the law, having become a curse for us (for it is written, "Cursed is everyone who hangs on a tree"), that the blessing of Abraham might come upon the Gentiles in Christ Jesus, that we might receive the promise of the Spirit through faith."

First, I want you to see from these verses that if you seek to be justified through works of the law you will be placed under a curse or bear a heavy burden. In other words, if you try to please God outside of faith, it is going to be harder than it should be. Let me show you the difference between being under the law and being under grace through this example. When I was much younger I learned how to water ski. At first, I remember being dragged around the lake, unable to stand up until someone told me what I was doing was wrong. I was told to let the movement of the boat pull me up, but instead I was trying to do it myself. Pulling myself up was actually causing me to fall. Finally, I stopped trying to pull myself up. I let the boat do the work and I was able to stand up right away. The act of attempting to do the work myself is a lot like being under the law. It's like trying to pull yourself up instead of letting God pull you up. If you are trying to obey God out of your own strength you will fail, but if you rely on His strength and His power it will pull you up every time.

The second thing I want you see from the above scripture is that Jesus became a curse for us in order that the blessing of Abraham would come upon us. What is a curse? It is a force which tries to dominate our lives; a force that attempts to keep us broke or sick, or in a place of lack. Jesus took on the curse so that it would no longer have the ability to control our lives.

The verses above speak of the blessings of Abraham. Deuteronomy 28 explains the blessings in detail, but let me summarize the blessing using the 13th verse.

Deuteronomy 28:13
"And the Lord will make you the head and not the tail; you shall be above only, and not be beneath, if you heed the commandments of the Lord your God, which I command you today, and are careful to observe them."

What does it mean to be the head and not the tail? Let me illustrate it this way. I have a little dog named Gracey. Whenever I come home, she looks up at me and wags her tail. Whenever she goes outside she exits the house head first. I've never seen her back out of her doggie door tail first with her little head following behind. The only way she can walk is head first with her tail at the back. Clearly, there is a difference in the parts that receive preference! If we are the head, we should be leading—*not* our circumstances.

The blessing of Abraham is a force which also has the power to control your circumstances in life, but it is one of peace, health, and provision. I remember years ago we had a pastor in our area who resigned because his wife was sick and they needed to move to a drier climate for her health. I admired his love for his wife, but I was also saddened that he did not realize the blessing of Abraham could have changed the situation he was in.

> **"Passing through a hard place is different than staking a claim to remain there."**

Think about all of the people who follow the Lord yet are not aware of the truth that has the ability to operate in their lives. People who work jobs they can't stand simply because they need the money, or live in places they don't like because they can't afford anything else. Please understand what I'm trying to communicate here: I am not saying that valleys in life are avoidable. We all travel through difficult valleys and rough roads. What I am saying is that you do not have to live in the valley. Passing through a hard place is different than staking a claim to remain there.

The third thing I want you to take away from these verses is that the curse of the law has been broken over you if you have accepted Jesus as Lord of your life.

We all have family trees. Sometimes when we talk about our family tree we'll joke and say that we've got a lot of fruits and nuts on it. But on a more serious note, some may say cancer runs in their family. Some families may have a history of mental illness, while others may have streaks of poverty. The Word of God tells us that we have been grafted into a new tree (Romans 11:17) and this is the family of God. Health, prosperity, peace, and joy run in your family now. You have a new family tree that stems from your Heavenly Father. Mental illness doesn't run in

His family; the mind of Christ is in operation. Sickness and disease do not run in His family because you've been healed by the stripes of Jesus. Victory of the Son is what runs through your family line now.

The curse of the law was broken when Jesus died on the cross. Two verses that support this are found in Isaiah 53:4, 5. It describes two kinds of sins for which Jesus had died: transgressions and iniquities. The sin of transgression can be described this way. It's as if someone violated a NO TRESPASSING sign by crossing over without permission. When a trespass occurs, it is an act that is not permitted. The sin of iniquity is different. In Hebrew, the word "iniquity" means *to bend or to distort.* Iniquity is repeated sin until it becomes a "bent" in life. These are the kinds of sins that create generational curses, with things like addiction that are passed down a family line. Jesus was bruised for our iniquities—those things which produced those generational curses. It is interesting to note that the word "bruised" is used to show what he endured for us regarding that type of sin. When you are bruised, that area stays discolored for a long time. A generational curse can last up to four generations (Exodus 20:5; Numbers 14:18; Deuteronomy 5:9). But Jesus bore these curses on the cross so we could be free from them.

Do you see how people can live in such a way that may prove to be harder than necessary? When we lack knowledge concerning what is ours in Christ, we may find our situations or circumstances heavier or more burdensome. I want to share how this was really the case for me years ago. When I came to the Lord, I had terrible allergies and I endured them for years. They were so bad that I needed to get shots every week for my condition. When I was younger I would go outside to play and I'd get a bloody nose if I played too roughly. My nose would also bleed if I was around dust or mold. My sinuses were a great source of irritation and pain for me. When I came to the Lord later on in life, I found the verse that explained that Jesus had redeemed us from these generational curses. I stood in faith for healing and after nine months of speaking the Word of God over my body, I was totally healed. Some people do not believe in healing without solid evidence. Twenty years after the Lord had healed me, I had a doctor test me for allergies and I was confirmed to have no allergies whatsoever. God heals but we must believe in His healing power.

With regard to your own life, I ask the question again: Could it be that following God is harder than it should be?

The blessings of Abraham give you dominion over your circumstances. In Christ, we no longer need reasons why we cannot live the abundant life God desires for us to live. There is no longer a reason why you cannot fulfill your dreams and purposes of God if you start believing today.

Chapter 7
Destroying the Power of Mistakes

Mistakes and past failures can create a huge burden we are not meant to carry. Once we come to the Lord and begin operating from a position of righteousness, living under the power of our mistakes from the past must disappear from our lives. I am going to show you how to destroy the power of mistakes and blunders and begin living in freedom from these burdens. What I mean by the word "power" is this: When mistakes are made, it has the ability to create guilt and regret. These can become a negative force, which, if not handled correctly, will produce a negative effect later in life. It is only through the truth of the gospel that we can put to rest all of those old regrets and bury them once and for all.

The first place we discover guilt, shame, and condemnation taking place in the Bible is right at the beginning, in Genesis chapter 3. Here, we read that Eve has partaken of the fruit from the forbidden tree, in the middle of the garden. She also gives some to her husband, who proceeds to eat it as well.

Genesis 3:7-10
"Then the eyes of both of them were opened, and they knew that they

were naked; and they sewed fig leaves together and made themselves coverings. And they heard the sound of the Lord God walking in the garden in the cool of the day, and Adam and his wife hid themselves from the presence of the Lord God among the trees of the garden. Then the Lord God called to Adam and said to him, "Where are you?" So he said, "I heard Your voice in the garden, and I was afraid because I was naked; and I hid myself.""

This was the act that had plunged mankind into death. The Bible states that the eyes of Adam and Eve were opened and they saw they were naked and hid themselves. Sin itself created shame and guilt, and it has been plaguing mankind ever since. We often think of guilt and shame as something God uses to keep us from sinning, but it was not there at creation; it came into existence as a result of sin.

The first thing Adam did after his disobedience toward God was to try to cover his nakedness with fig leaves. In a similar way, we try to cover ourselves with our own righteousness or goodness. Later, after speaking with Adam, God covered him and Eve with the skin of an animal. Blood was shed to provide for them a proper covering. It was a type of covering that would eventually point to the true covering we receive by the shed blood of Jesus. The blood of Jesus has clothed us with a robe of righteousness.

> **"We often think of guilt and shame as something God uses to keep us from sinning, but it was not there at creation; it came into existence as a result of sin. "**

Here is what I feel many well-meaning people do who are ignorant of this truth: They use the wrong means to get positive results in their lives. These people use guilt and shame as means to "living right." This tactic reminds me of a businessman who desires to provide for his family, but he uses lying and cheating to accomplish his goals. His desire is good, it's well-meaning, but the means are corrupt. Or take an athlete who uses performance-enhancing drugs to win a competition; there's nothing wrong with winning, but winning through cheating doesn't count.

The generation in which I grew up were heavy users of the guilt and shame methods of getting results. The use of *Shame on you* and *You should feel bad for* (fill in the blank) were heard regularly. Perhaps mostly done with good intentions, it is still the wrong means to produce proper results. It produces destruction. Guilt does nothing but create regret, and that negative power is what destroys confidence and potential.

Don't Breed Guilt

Have you ever known parents who used guilt to get their children to do or say the right things? I want to tell you there is a better way to awaken possibilities and great potential in children. Life filled with guilt and shame is one that brings with it destruction and strained relationships. Have you ever wondered why sometimes preachers' kids are notorious for bad behavior? I personally believe it could possibly be due to guilt and shame they have been made to feel, even in their own home. Perhaps their pastor/fathers would personally use them in sermon illustrations!

The best way to deal with bad behavior is not to ignore it, but to reveal that it is wrong. What you say and how you say it makes all the difference to the heart and mind of a child. We should point out wrong-doing, and we can even point out that certain actions are far below Christ-like behavior, or that what was done was a shameful thing, but that is not the same as using tactics as shame and guilt to point out imperfections.

In the first chapter of this book, I had touched on the subject of sin consciousness. I want to expand on that further now that we have a good foundation through which we can understand this concept.

I don't believe brothers and sisters in Christ should have sin consciousness operating in their lives. The more conscious one is of sin in his life, the greater the tendency is to sin. On the contrary, the more conscious a person is of righteousness operating in his life, the more he will act like a truly righteous person.

The Slippery Bank of Sin

Sin is like a slippery bank. You don't just fall into sin, just like you don't fall into a river unless you're standing too close to the edge. I have found this to be the case in my own life whenever I mess up. It first starts by being on the bank. Falling into sin starts with standing at the bank, in this case that bank is guilt. It might start with someone trying to condemn me for something I'd said, or reminding me of some regretful thing I'd done in the past. I know if I don't handle this type of situation correctly, it's easy to start playing the blame game instead of taking responsibility for myself. Think about Adam, when he ate the forbidden fruit. Instead of accepting his role in wrongdoing, he actually said it was God's fault indirectly by giving him the woman, and Eve directly by pointing out she gave it to him. Guilt can really keep us going down the wrong path.

I'd like to point out here that you can even do seemingly good things out of guilt. Guilt can motivate you to go to church, or pray every day. You can even serve or give financially out of guilt, but all that does is awaken blame and justification in your life. Being motivated by guilt causes us to live in a compromising manner and ultimately do things that aren't pleasing to God.

Feeling bad about sin does not cause people to stop sinning in their life; it is believing in the gift of righteousness which keeps them from habitual sin. Why is it that the more aware we are of sin, the easier it is to continue to be tempted by it? The reason is because somewhere down the road we depended on ourselves and our own strength to fight temptation—not on the finished work of Christ. The more we depend on ourselves, the more strength we hand over to sin! This is why the scriptures speak of denying oneself, for this is the key to living victoriously. It is trusting in what Christ has done for us rather than trusting ourselves. Look at the apostle, Peter. He denied the Lord three times. On the Passover night before Jesus was handed over to the Romans, he told his disciples they would be scattered like sheep without a shepherd. Peter, full of self-confidence, basically said he wasn't like the others, and even went so far as to say, "Even if all are made to stumble because of you, I will never be made to stumble!" and, "Even if I have to die with you, I will not deny you!" (Matthew 26:33, 35). Did you catch the "I's" in Peter replies? If only he had said something like, *Lord, with your help, I won't deny you* perhaps the turnout would have been different!

Feeding Two Dogs

When I first started out in the faith, I was told there are two people in you at all times: the old man and the new man. I was taught that the one you feed the most will be the one who prevails, much like two dogs—the one who receives the most food will be the strongest of the two. But the Bible doesn't teach that. It teaches your "old man" has passed away and the "new man" is alive in your heart.

> *Romans 6:6, 7*
> *"...knowing this, that our old man was crucified with Him, that the body of sin might be done away with, that we should no longer be slaves of sin. For he who has died has been freed from sin."*

Whenever we focus on our sin it gives strength to the flesh. What we should do instead is focus in on the new man in Christ living within us. When we do this, the power of Christ is released over our lives.

Stop Digging Up the Dead

If we are always trying to dig up the old man or things like past sin and old behaviors that belong with the old man, we will experience a constant struggle to remain in faith for anything in our lives. Once you are saved, you need to continually remind yourself of the forgiveness you received through Jesus. As you journey on through life, the accuser of the brethren, Satan, will tell you that you're not deserving of this blessing or that blessing. Remind him that God will not hold you accountable for those sins he tries to bring to your remembrance because He has held Jesus accountable for them instead. (You can really get to the devil by reminding him that God will certainly hold him accountable for all he's done and there is coming a day when an angel will be ordered to throw him into the abyss!)

A perfect example of one who operated in the full forgiveness of God's grace was the apostle Paul. In one of his epistles, he had even written he had wronged no one (2 Corinthians 7:2). If we look into Paul's past, the truth was that he had stood by as a witness holding the garments of those who had stoned Stephen to death, the first martyr for Christ. He received a letter from the high priest directing him to arrest people who professed the Lord Jesus, persecuted them, and incarcerated them. But yet, years after his encounter with Jesus on the road to Damascus, he was able to say with all confidence that he had "wronged no man." If God forgets our past, then we should, too.

Questions to Ponder

If God has removed all guilt from our lives, what then creates the feeling that we are somehow still to be found guilty? Since we have been forgiven, why is it that we oftentimes find it hard to forgive ourselves?

I believe the reason is simple: If you continually believe you must do something to earn the right to be forgiven, then you will have a difficult time forgiving yourself. Guilt will have no place in your life if you remember that guilt cannot exist in the one who freely receives God's forgiveness.

Take, for instance, two people working in the same position at a company. One worker puts in his normal 40-hour work week, but sometimes he comes in late and leaves early. He never puts in any overtime and doesn't ever think to work longer than is minimally required. Now the other worker is completely opposite; he shows up early and almost always works late into the evening. He goes well above and beyond his obligations. At the end of the year, the boss decides he's going to give out bonuses. Both workers receive $1,000 bonus each. When the worker who put in all those extra hours discovers that his co-worker received the same amount, he's indignant because he doesn't believe it's fair. But what the first worker didn't take into account was that it was at the boss' discretion that they received anything at all.

Grace operates in the same way. At God's discretion, we are all given equal opportunity to receive and walk in His grace, without the need to earn or work for it. The one who feels guilty about sin or failures is the one who feels the need to earn God's grace.

Easily Offended

I have known many people who have come to my church because they were offended by someone or something that occurred in another church. Unfortunately, most of these people end up developing a list of things they feel are wrong within the church until they finally leave. Why are some people more easily offended or fault-finding than others? Is it within their DNA or is it something else?

I believe there's only one reason why people are more easily offended than others. I believe it's because these people are trying to do something to earn forgiveness. If they live in this state they begin living under guilt. When you live free from guilt, you don't feel the need to blame or find fault with others. Guilt is such a negative force which stays with you unless it is destroyed by the power of forgiveness. Living under the weight of guilt drags you down and hinders what you can accomplish for the Lord.

Everything He Is!

I want you to remember this very important point. Everything Jesus is, so am I and so are you! But everything I've done and everything you've done has nothing to do with who he is. That statement is so important, I want you to read that again: everything we've ever done whether good or bad has no effect on who Jesus is. But as he is so are we in this world!

Seeing ourselves in this proper light is the key to great success, for it causes us to see ourselves as big, not small in life. When we realize that we are big in Christ, experiencing great successes will keep us in a place of humility, not pride because we know it is through Jesus that we can do all things. What a wonderful gift God has given us in Christ. Let Jesus be big in your life and rejoice!

Chapter 8
Judging Yourself Correctly

So many opportunities are missed by those who have judged themselves unworthy of the many blessings God desires to bestow on them. Some people think that others may deserve God's best, but not them. It's this kind of thinking which causes some to also believe they were born "on the wrong side of the tracks." With this thinking also comes thoughts that believe they don't have the right education or the proper social status to obtain certain blessings or favor.

All this boils down to one question. Do you judge yourself unworthy to receive the blessings of God?

Satan never deceives us by simply telling us a lie—he always mixes it with truth. Just as some evil person would poison a dog, they'd never do it by trying to just give the dog pure poison. They'd hide it in a piece of meat or something equally tasty. Satan knows it's a fruitless pursuit for the person who is trying to gain access to God's blessing by establishing their own sense of worthiness.

It is true that within ourselves we are not worthy to receive anything from

God, but if you believed on Christ, you are found in him. His worthiness gives us access to receive everything from God.

Acts 13:45, 46
"But when the Jews saw the multitudes, they were filled with envy; and contradicting and blaspheming, they opposed the things spoken by Paul. Then Paul and Barnabas grew bold and said, "It was necessary that the word of God should be spoken to you first; but since you reject it, and judge yourselves unworthy of everlasting life, behold, we turn to the Gentiles."

The self-righteousness of the Jews prevented them from feeling worthy to freely receive salvation. They judged themselves as unworthy. This still happens even today. Many judge themselves as unworthy and therefore unable to receive from God.

It's Always About Him

See, the moment you begin thinking, *I need to become worthy enough to receive from God* is the moment you'll begin doing things which will prevent God's grace from operating in your life. I believe in being a doer of the Word, but I don't believe in putting myself under the works of the law in attempts to somehow become worthy.

Romans 4:16
"Therefore it is of faith that it might be according to grace, so that the promise might be sure to all the seed, not only to those who are of the law, but also to those who are of the faith of Abraham, who is the father of us all..."

When God Calls

Does God go out and choose all the A students before he calls people to salvation? Does He choose the best behaved or the highest achiever? His choices are never based on any of those qualifications. In fact, His grace allows for everyone to have the ability to receive from Him. From the drug addict to the business man—and everyone below, in between, and above—can receive His grace because it is based on Jesus' worthiness, not ours.

I wonder how many peoples' lives would be transformed if they started believing who they are in Christ? Our identity in Christ builds us up and never tears us down; it gives us assurance and confidence when we are able to solely rely on him. It makes us strong when we put his armor on. Putting on the full armor of God reminds me of the character Iron Man. He's different than Superman because he's just a regular human without his suit. Superman is always supernaturally strong, whether he's wearing a tie or a cape. We're more like Iron Man in this way because in order for us to become supernaturally strong, we need to put on our "Iron Man" suit—of course in our case, it's putting on the full armor of God. No wonder the Bible tells us to "be strong in the Lord and in the power of his might" (Ephesians 6:10). It does not say to *be strong in yourself and in the power of your human strength.* We are called to completely rely on Christ.

When we begin thinking like someone under the law, we are relying in our own strength to receive blessings. This type of self-reliance is like kryptonite to the believer. Why? Because it actually weakens the supernatural strength we possess through Christ. This is why Paul continued to teach that if we are led by the Spirit we are no longer under the law. Power is restored when we rely on Jesus instead of ourselves. Suppose receiving from God was based on our works, or how good we were. That would certainly go against the following scripture.

Philippians 3:12
"Not that I have already attained, or am already perfected; but I press on, that I may lay hold of that for which Christ Jesus has also laid hold of me."

Paul himself said he had not reached perfection but he still pressed on. Think about how he had been in faith for years, wrote one third of the entire New Testament, and yet proclaimed he had not "arrived." The good news is that how far we go in life is not determined by what we can see, for it is all based on the worthiness of Jesus.

Many people judge themselves unworthy of God's best because they don't consider themselves to be perfect. Do you know what spiritual maturity is? It's not about reaching a certain level in Christianity, but it is constantly being in the process of reaching higher, pursuing God to a greater degree. Even a new believer in Christ can be considered mature if he is reaching for more of God.

What is "Unworthiness?"

What does "unworthiness" mean? It is the feeling that keeps one believing that he or she does not merit the level of blessing received, or general feelings of inadequacy which keeps one from pursuing goals, dreams, or desires. Performance-driven people may seem to be highly motivated, but some often try to work for the blessing of God because of this feeling of unworthiness. They may pray long and hard to be heard; they may serve endlessly in order to somehow be deserving of blessings. Praying and serving are, of course, wonderful to do, but if performance-driven people desire for those works to be accepted before God, they do not have to act on the Word to be worthy; they should do those things according to the Word because they have already been made worthy. Since God Himself has qualified us, we are able to do many things we could not accomplish before in life. The person who understands that Jesus has made them acceptable before God is capable to do whatever He has called them to do. Consider the words in this next verse.

> *Mark 11:24*
> *"Therefore I say to you, whatever things you ask when you pray, believe that you receive them, and you shall have them."*

Think about it for a moment. This verse does not say, *Whatever things you desire for which you are worthy, believe you receive and you shall have it.* No, it says whatever things you desire simply believe that you receive it.

Here's another verse I find that sheds a wonderful light on our worthiness based on Christ.

> *Revelation 5:9*
> *"And they sang a new song, saying:*
> *'You are worthy to take the scroll,*
> *And to open its seals;*
> *For You were slain,*
> *And have redeemed us to God by Your blood*
> *Out of every tribe and tongue and people and nation...'"*

The four living creatures who stand before God and the 24 elders seated around the throne were singing this new song. It is clear this new song in heaven was about Jesus and his worthiness; that it was he who was able to make us worthy before God. This is so powerful! Now look what it says in the fourth chapter.

Revelation 4:9
"Whenever the living creatures give glory and honor and thanks to Him who sits on the throne, who lives forever and ever, the twenty-four elders fall down before Him who sits on the throne and worship Him who lives forever and ever, and cast their crowns before the throne..."

This is one of my favorite verses in the Bible because I can just envision everyone in heaven fully aware that their rewards are based on the worthiness of Jesus. Those crowns that the 24 elders had received as a result of their works in life were based on the work of Jesus, not their own. That truth caused them to fall to their knees and throw their crowns before the feet of the One who made them worthy. None would dare take any credit for himself. Hallelujah!

Jesus' worthiness will open doors for your healing; it will open for you doors of prosperity. It will open for you doors of deliverance from oppression and frustration. Jesus' worthiness will open doors for you that you never dreamed possible.

True Humility

Some people equate the definition of humility with the feeling of being unworthy, but that is biblically wrong. Humility is not feeling unworthy; it is submitting yourself to God's will and purposes in your life.

As I was praying recently, the Lord spoke to me about someone in our church. He told me that He had far more for that individual than what that person was believing God had for him. I believe when we understand the truth about what really makes us worthy before God, we will be able to do far more than we ever thought possible in the Lord.

So many things can prevent us from feeling unworthy or undeserving of the Lord, and this prevents our faith from embracing opportunities and dreams and acting on them. I am here to tell you that God has something bigger for your life than you think He does.

This truth reminds me of a story I heard once. A little boy was in a store, staring at a jar of candy on the cashier's counter. The owner of the store saw the little boy eyeing the candy and told him to go ahead and take some. The boy just continued to stare, not saying a thing. The owner once again encouraged him to take some candy from the jar, and again the boy did nothing but stare at the treats. Finally, the owner reached in and pulled a handful of candy from the jar and encouraged the little boy to open up his hands. The boy smiled and told the man, "Your hands can take a lot more out of the candy jar than mine." I really like this visual because I can't help but think that God's got so much more in store for us than we can hold!

> *Ephesians 3:20*
> *"Now to Him who is able to do exceedingly abundantly above all that we ask or think, according to the power that works in us, to Him be glory in the church by Christ Jesus to all generations, forever and ever. Amen."*

Faith in Jesus

Here is something which will help you release your faith in God to a great measure. Remember to put your faith in Him, not through your own faith, but by entrusting that faith to Jesus. It is all about putting our faith on the One who is faithful. The more you grasp that, the more fruit you will see produced in your life.

> *Romans 8:31,32*
> *"What then shall we say to these things? If God is for us, who can be against us? He who did not spare His own Son, but delivered Him up for us all, how shall He not with Him also freely give us all things?"*

When I read the above verse, two thoughts come to my mind: that Jesus is the lamb without blemish, and that he who knew no sin was made sin for us that we might become the righteousness of God in him (2 Corinthians 5:21). If Jesus had any sin in his life at all, he could not have been the perfect sacrifice for mankind, nor would he have been worthy of being exalted above every name. Since he was the perfect sacrifice worthy of every blessing from God, those of us who place our trust in him are entitled to receive from God. If you need healing in your life, ask yourself, *Is Jesus worthy of healing?* If the answer is yes, then it applies to you, too. Whatever grace you need over your life, you can receive it because Jesus is worthy.

If we believe correctly, it will cause us to ask from God without limitation. It will cause us to move in the direction of greatness in our lives. We simply must believe these truths and judge ourselves worthy of all that Christ died to give us. True faith will always move us in the right direction.

Chapter 9
The Chastening of the Lord

Does God chasten us with sickness, disease, or by inflicting premature death? The word "chasten" is the Greek word *paideuo*. The definition of this word means *to train up a child, i.e. educate, discipline, correct, instruct.* If, according to Matthew 7:11, our Heavenly Father gives us good things to those who ask of Him, and is able to bless us in a greater way than an earthly father who has a sin nature, why would we think that He puts sickness or disease upon us if we sin?

Our society has laws governing child abuse. Why do we think that God would abuse His children with poverty, sickness, and even physical death? The best way to understand the Father's love toward us is to study the life of Jesus and his ministry. Never did Jesus put sickness or inflict premature death upon anyone. If fact, in Acts 10:38, the Bible says that "God anointed Jesus of Nazareth with the Holy Spirit and with power and went about doing good, healing all who were oppressed by the devil because God was with Him." The Bible clearly states that Jesus went about healing all who were oppressed by the devil. This proves that God did not chasten people by employing methods of sickness and disease. Jesus would have been going against the Father's form of discipline if that were the case. The truth is that Jesus displayed the very nature of the Father and His love toward us when he came into the world.

I believe if we rightly divide the Word, all these misconceptions will disappear from our lives. One very important area that is often misconstrued has to do with communion and judgment. Let's read 1 Corinthians 11:27-33 and examine what the scriptures say about it.

> *1 Corinthians 11:27-32*
> *"Therefore whoever eats this bread or drinks this cup of the Lord in an unworthy manner will be guilty of the body and blood of the Lord. But let a man examine himself, and so let him eat of the bread and drink of the cup. For he who eats and drinks in an unworthy manner eats and drinks judgment to himself, not discerning the Lord's body. For this reason many are weak and sick among you, and many sleep. For if we would judge ourselves, we would not be judged. But when we are judged, we are chastened by the Lord, that we may not be condemned with the world."*

> **"The Bible clearly states that Jesus went about healing all who were oppressed by the devil. This proves that God did not chasten people by employing methods of sickness and disease. Jesus would have been going against the Father's form of discipline if that were the case."**

Perhaps you have attended church services in which the pastor, prior to communion, told the congregation to "examine your heart" and make sure no sin was present. Because of this, communion time became associated with searching for sin. This is completely contrary to the actual teaching in scripture. As I've explained many times in the previous chapters, we are to remove sin consciousness, not develop it, in our lives.

One of the first things I'd like to note about these verses is the use of the expression, "unworthy manner." The verse is not saying you need to make sure you are not unworthy; what Paul was stating is that you must take communion in the manner and purpose for which it was designed. If people took communion and simply viewed it as something like eating another meal or a snack, that would be taking it in an unworthy manner. When we partake of communion we must discern the Lord's body, but what does that mean? To understand this, we must first read the following verse.

Isaiah 53:5
"But He was wounded for our transgressions,
He was bruised for our iniquities;
The chastisement for our peace was upon Him,
And by His stripes we are healed."

The Bible is clear that it was Jesus who fulfilled this prophecy. Therefore, when we discern the body of Christ, we discern (or make the distinction) that Jesus has provided healing by dying on the cross for us.

Another portion of scripture concerning communion that we need to look at is verse 30, " . . . for this reason many are weak and sick among you, and many sleep . . . " As far as I know, this is the only scripture that tells us the reason why people are sick and weakly, and that some die prematurely. Paul is saying that it is because there are those who do not discern the body and blood of the Lord Jesus Christ.

Many people interpret this the opposite way and say the reason why there are those who are sick is because they do not judge themselves concerning sin in their lives. I remember once during a service I had noticed that one of our church leaders was not taking communion. I found out later he had sin in his life and he thought that if he did not participate in communion that he would not be judged for what he was covering up. Now, do you suppose if that were true, we could all just never take communion and go out and live wildly with no consequences? Views such as this are what keep people out of church. They figure that if they just stay out of church, then God won't judge them for sins, especially if they steer clear of communion. That kind of thinking is the same that would reason if someone is taking illegal drugs, he certainly wouldn't be going down to the police station and have a chat with the police chief while he's high. But this is wrong thinking where God is concerned. God gives us grace so that we can be reconciled to Him. Remember, He has already placed judgment onto Jesus for our sin so He can forgive the sinner.

Because many people misinterpret these sections of scripture, it causes some to pre-judge others if there is sickness or weakness in their lives. But these verses were not written to give us a way to judge people. These verses are to teach us the importance of remembering Christ's sacrifice and to acknowledge the blood and body of Jesus. When we partake of communion, we must remember that healing is provided in the atonement. This will drive out sickness and prolong life.

Now let us look at the last portion of those verses regarding communion, verses 31 and 32.

1 Corinthians 11:31, 32
"For if we would judge ourselves, we would not be judged. But when we are judged, we are chastened by the Lord, that we may not be condemned with the world."

The first time the word "judge" is used in this text, it is the same word used for "discern," as in discerning the Lord's body. The Greek word is *diakrino*, and is used in the imperfect tense, speaking of an action which is not completed. In other words, if we discerned and recognized that the body and blood of Jesus heals, then judgment would not occur. The text continues, saying, "...when we are judged, we are chastened by the Lord..."

The word "chasten," as I noted previously, means *to train or correct.* Let me give you two contemporary examples of the meaning to "chasten" since this is not an everyday word in our vocabulary. It's freezing outside and your child is preparing to run out of the house without a coat. You stop your kid and firmly tell him he must put on a coat before leaving the house because you don't want him catching a cold. Or perhaps you've made dinner and your child pushes away all the green vegetables. You tell him he can't leave the table until all those vegetables are eaten because they're good for him.

To chasten simply means to properly train, as in raising a child. When we understand the definition, then it is clear that God chastens us for the purpose of training so that we would "not be condemned with the world." The world in this case refers to those who do not confess Jesus as Lord. "The world" is constantly in a state of sickness and disease; "the world" often experiences premature death. To summarize what Paul is saying in 1 Corinthians 11:27-32, he explains that we are not to take communion like a regular meal, for if we do, we will be judged (chastened), and judging is beneficial because it is designed to spare us from the trouble that others in world experience. Praise God for His love!

Jesus condemned the action of judging a person's spiritual life based on one's outward condition of health. Let's look in John chapter 9.

John 9:1-5
"Now as Jesus passed by, He saw a man who was blind from birth. And His disciples asked Him, saying, 'Rabbi, who sinned, this man or his parents, that he was born blind?' Jesus answered, 'Neither this man nor his parents sinned, but that the works of God should be revealed in him. I must work the works of Him who sent Me while it is day; the night is coming when no one can work. As long as I am in the world, I am the light of the world.'"

Jewish leaders concluded that the man who was born blind must have either sinned, or that his parents had sinned, causing this handicap. Jesus straightened out his own disciples in the presence of the blind man. Why? I believe he did it in the man's presence so he could have the faith to be healed. This man must have heard many times before that it was either he or his parents who had sinned because when the man was brought to the Pharisees and he testified that Jesus was sent from God and was healed, the religious leaders said, "You were born in sins, and you are teaching us?"

Even when sin opened the door for sickness to enter, Jesus never brought up the issue of sin until after he healed the person. Do you remember the story of the man in John 5 who had been sick for 38 years, who laid every day at the pool of Bethesda? Jesus asked the man if he wanted to be made well, and after he healed him, told him to, "Sin no more, lest a worse thing come upon you." We find the same approach in the epistles. James 5:14,15 states, "Is any among you sick? Let him call for the elders of the church, and let them pray over him anointing him with oil in the name of the Lord and the prayer of faith will save the sick and the Lord will raise him up. And if he has committed any sins, he will be forgiven."

It is clear from scripture that the Lord heals first, then deals with the issue of sin. Do you see how we have held a wrong view of our Heavenly Father regarding sin and death instead of seeing Him in the light of grace and mercy?

I used to ask myself, *In the parables that Jesus taught, why did he always use the comparison of "evil" men to our Heavenly Father?* For example, in Matthew 7:11, where Jesus states, "If you then being evil, know how to give good gifts to your children, how much more will your Father who is in heaven give good things to those who ask him?" I believe it's clear that Jesus used these examples because men do not see God in the right light. People often think of God being cruel, harsh, and overbearing when in fact He is not like that at all. He loves us unconditionally. Faith is weakened when others conceal God's love or show Him in an improper light. Unfortunately, there will be many in the end times who will be deceived into thinking that God is different than who He actually is.

Chapter 10
God's Grace and the Rapture

I want to discuss a topic that we have not yet explored regarding grace, and that is how Christians should view the event we call "the rapture." I believe that a majority of people within the church have an inaccurate view of God's love toward them when it comes to end-time teaching. The return of the Lord is a concern for many, and I want to shed light on this matter so that we would be eager to prepare for His coming, rather than fearful of the future.

If end-time teaching were taught correctly, I believe it would lead to a financial increase of giving within the church because people would understand the need to take the gospel out to a dying world. I believe people would be much more active and resolute to intercede for their families and do those things that would be uncomfortable in order to see the salvation of friends and loved ones. People would have a greater urgency to win many more souls to Christ.

To illustrate why we must have a greater urgency to reach people at this important time, let me give you the following example. Let's say one day you are driving your car. You are up on a hill and can see that hundreds of yards below a bridge had gone out that reached over to your side. From the other side of the bridge, drivers can't see the danger ahead because they don't have your vantage point. You get out of your vehicle because you can see cars up ahead preparing to cross onto the bridge. You wave your hands in the air frantically. Now you see a vehicle that looks like it belongs to one of your best friends. You can't cross the bridge, but you start honking your horn, shouting, and jumping up and down because you want to do all you can to warn him of the impending danger. How much more should we be concerned for our friends and loved ones now that the return of Jesus is closer than ever before?

Hebrews 9:28
"...so Christ was offered once to bear the sins of many. To those who eagerly wait for Him He will appear a second time, apart from sin, for salvation."

Jesus will return "apart from sin" because the issue of sin had been resolved prior to his return. This means two things: first, those who have died before his coming have already been forgiven; and second, those who are alive at his coming have also already been forgiven of their sins: past, present, and future. It is very clear that Jesus' one-time sacrifice removed God's wrath upon sin from the believer once and for all.

> **"Whenever God's grace is removed from end-time teaching and is replaced with some form of fear, it fails to produce true preparation for the return of Jesus."**

This means that when I sin, it doesn't cost me my salvation, but it could cost me eternal rewards if I continue down the wrong path. As a believer in Christ, sin will never cost me my salvation, praise God. The believers who will stand before the judgment seat of Christ will be judged for their works, not for their sin because that price had already been fully paid by Jesus. (We will further discuss the judgment seat of Christ and the great white throne of judgment in a later chapter.)

The reason why it is important to understand this concept is because many people feel condemned by their own actions, which prevent them from actually moving on to accomplish work for God's kingdom. If we feel constantly condemned, our motivation to pursue godly things is minimal. We must understand God's grace for these last days so that we can be productive and pursue God's purposes at this very crucial time in history.

Another point I want to bring out concerning the rapture of the church is the timing at which Jesus will remove his bride from the earth. Although scripture tells us that no one will know the day or hour of the Son's return, the broader placement of the event is not hard to determine when we are able to grasp God's great love for us. Remember, He will never pour His wrath upon you once you are saved, for He unleashed all that wrath upon His Son at the cross on your behalf.

Pre-Trib, Mid-Trib, Post-Trib?

There seems to be a lot of confusion about Jesus' return. Some people hold what is called a "pre-tribulation" view, meaning, a catching away of the church before the great tribulation (noted in Matthew 24:21). Others believe in a "mid-tribulation" position, meaning the rapture taking place midway through a seven year period (Revelation 13:5-8). Still others share a "post-tribulation" perspective, meaning they believe they will endure a time of persecution that will conclude with the rapture taking place afterward (Matthew 24:29, 30). There are also those who hold a "pan-tribulation" view, meaning no matter when the event of the rapture takes place, it will all just "pan out" in the end.

Let me give you just a few simple reasons why I believe the body of Christ will be caught up before the time of the great tribulation. One is in reference to Matthew 24:36; 42-44, part of which I just paraphrased above.

Matthew 24:36, 37
"But of that day and hour no one knows, not even the angels of heaven, but My Father only. But as the days of Noah were, so also will the coming of the Son of Man be."

vv. 42-44
"Watch therefore, for you do not know what hour your Lord is coming. But know this, that if the master of the house had known what hour the thief would come, he would have watched and not allowed his house to be broken into. Therefore you also be ready, for the Son of Man is

coming at an hour you do not expect."

A reason why it would be problematic to be raptured midway or after the tribulation is because we would know the time and hour of Jesus' coming. If the event takes place in the middle of the great tribulation, we would know that period lasts seven years. The seven-year count would begin when the antichrist signs a peace treaty with Israel, so that would make the Lord's return imminent at the three-and-a-half year mark. The only way we would not know the day and hour of his coming is if the event were to take place before the start of the tribulation.

If Jesus even told his own disciples that he would return at a time when they did not expect, and they were the ones who wrote the very scriptures concerning his return, what would make us think we would know of his exact return? There is a reason why the return of the Lord is compared to the times of Noah. When Noah entered the ark and the flood came and lifted him and his family above the water, the waters receded and the ark rested upon the earth once again. So it will also be with the rapture. We will be taken up, and when the tribulation recedes, we will come back down with Jesus.

Why does God keep this period of time such a secret? I believe He does this out of love for His children in a similar way an earthly father might treat his child. Let's say it was the child's first visit to the dentist. If you were the parent, you wouldn't tell your child about going to the dentist a month before the appointment and then tell them the horrors of sitting in the dentist chair. You wouldn't tell your child about what happens when a cavity is found or the sound and smell of the drill when the dentist has your mouth cranked open, making way for a filling. You certainly wouldn't remind them repeatedly a week before the appointment that the day is nearing. No. You'd probably just pick your child up from school and say, "We're going to see a nice man who going to give you some candy while he looks at your teeth." Do you understand my point? God doesn't want us to "freak out" about the future. He wants you to live each day to its fullest. He conceals this day out of His great love for us.

Is There a Partial Rapture?

Let me further aid you in removing fear of this question of timing by posing this next question and giving you my best answer. When the rapture happens, are believers who are "not living right" going to be left behind?

1 Thessalonians 4:16-18
"For the Lord Himself will descend from heaven with a shout, with the voice of an archangel, and with the trumpet of God. And the dead in Christ will rise first. Then we who are alive and remain shall be caught up together with them in the clouds to meet the Lord in the air. And thus we shall always be with the Lord. Therefore comfort one another with these words."

We learn from this passage that believers who had died prior to the rapture will be resurrected first; then those who are alive at the time of this event will be caught away to join the Lord and the saints. We can conclude that those believers, even though some will not be "living right" or "perfectly right with God" at the time of the rapture will also be caught away because remember, Jesus' sacrifice already paid the price for sin at his first coming. His second coming is not about sin, but salvation. This means that those believers who were in a state of backsliding will go up. It means that those who have professed Christ yet harbored some form of unforgiveness in their hearts will go up. Why would we think God would exclude those living in similar conditions who are alive at His coming?

1 Thessalonians 5:9
"For God did not appoint us to wrath, but to obtain salvation through our Lord Jesus Christ, who died for us, that whether we wake or sleep, we should live together with Him."

The word "appoint" in the Greek is *tithémi* which means *to experience or to make one subject to something.* God has not appointed us to experience wrath in our lives. Once you are saved you never have to fear that you will be left behind.

I want to share briefly on a subject we will cover in more detail in another chapter, and that is the subject of repentance. Most people think they are going to hell because of their sins, but the truth is it will be because of their rejection of Jesus as their Savior. God knows we are sinners by nature, which is why He provided for us a Savior who had the power to forgive us of all our sins and give us the gift of righteousness. His gift of righteousness transforms sinners into saints. One reason that keeps people in this state of mind (believing that they will go to hell because of their sins), is because we often do not grasp the true meaning of repentance.

I was raised in a church where most people equated repentance to ceasing from sin, but that is not a correct view of the act of repentance. What is the true definition? Repentance is turning to God. It is not an end in itself, it is only a means through which God helps us. God is fully aware we cannot change without Him, so when we turn to Him, He enables us to truly change.

In my opinion, this whole idea of being left behind is built on faith by works rather than faith by the finished work of Christ. God does not only rapture those who live perfectly right, for none of us would qualify.

The Coming of the Lord

2 Thessalonians 2:1-3
"Now, brethren, concerning the coming of our Lord Jesus Christ and our gathering together to Him, we ask you, not to be soon shaken in mind or troubled, either by spirit or by word or by letter, as if from us, as though the <u>day of Christ</u> had come. Let no one deceive you by any means; for that Day will not come unless the <u>falling away comes first, and the man of sin is revealed, the son of perdition</u> . . ." (underline emphasis added)

In the church at the time the above text was written, many of the believers were upset because there was a teaching that was circulating, proclaiming that the day of the Lord had come, and that the day of wrath had arrived. This was very troubling to those in the church because Paul had already made it clear in his previous letter to them that God had delivered them (the church) from judgment and wrath (1 Thessalonians 1:10; 5:9). They were not troubled because they thought they had missed the rapture, for Paul and the apostles were still present. If anyone would have been raptured, certainly it would have been them.

Take note of the second time the word "Christ" is used in the passage. Although the Greek word used is Christos, meaning the Lord, the better word would have been Kurios (which also means Lord, but in a different context.) I'll tell you why Kurios would have been the more proper translation. The term Christos is used mostly to describe the Messiah, or the Anointed One, referring to Jesus as Savior. But the word Kurios is always used in connection to a time of judgment or wrath. Acts 2:20, 1 Corinthians 5:5, 2 Peter 2:9 all describe events surrounding "the day of the Lord," using this word. None of these events use the word "Lord" in terms of a Savior. Therefore, the use of the word conveying the term "Messiah" in 2 Thessalonians 2:2 is inaccurate in that it is describing the same event detailed in these other verses. Paul was telling the Thessalonians not to be troubled in mind or spirit because the (wrathful) day of the Lord had not yet come.

Throughout the rest of the chapter, Paul continues to remove fear of being left on earth during the great tribulation. He establishes that two things must first take place before the day of judgment arrives. First, that there must be a great "falling away," and that the antichrist is revealed. The term "falling away" means to rebel or to engage in insurrection. It is used in a passive sense, which tells us that this great falling away occurs due to an outside force.

The Holy Spirit had illuminated this scripture to me as I was reading it one day and I think you will really be blessed by this revelation as well. Prior to this revelation, I had always considered the great falling away and the revealing of the son of perdition as two separate and distinct events, rather than one. For example, if I told you I wanted you to wash the dishes first then dry them with a towel, I would be talking about one event (washing the dishes) with two distinct aspects to fulfilling the request (washing and drying). As I began to ponder what event would cause this great falling away and revealing of the antichrist, I realized it is the rapture of the church. Imagine what this planet will be like with not one believer here to intercede for the lost, or to pray for the government once the church is gone. Literally all of hell is going to break out, for we are the force (the church inhabited by the Holy Spirit) is what holds things together on the earth. Consider this as you read the following verse.

2 Thessalonians 2:6-8
"And now you know <u>what is restraining</u>, that he may be revealed in his own time. For the mystery of lawlessness is already at work; <u>only He who now restrains will do so until He is taken out of the way.</u> And then the lawless one will be revealed, whom the Lord will consume with the breath of His mouth and destroy with the brightness of His coming."
(underline emphasis added)

Paul uses the Greek word *ginomia* to describe the term taken "out of the way" in the above scripture. It means *to make a change of location in space*. The literal translation means moving from one place to another. This is exactly what the church will do at the time of the rapture: it will move from the earthly realm to the spiritual realm.

I believe one of the reasons why Paul did not mention the body of Christ directly in this text is because he would have been concerned his letter could be intercepted by the Roman authorities who would come to the false conclusion that the church was working against their laws and government.

Before we leave the topic of the rapture, I want to leave you with this illustration that will serve as a loving reminder of God's grace concerning His children.

The Story of the Elderly Woman

There was an elderly woman who lived in a broken down home. This home was so old, that there wasn't even any power hooked up to it! One day, a developer began knocking on the doors of this old neighborhood, telling the residents that these homes were going to be torn down to make way for a brand new complex he intended to build there. He sent one of his foremen to this elderly woman's home and offered her a high price for her lot. Although it was a good sum of money, she struggled with the idea and said, "I don't know if I can accept your offer. I've been here for so long and I'm just not comfortable with it." The foreman returned to the developer and told him what the woman said.

The developer decided to talk personally with the woman, and told her that if she sold the house to him he would build her a brand new home up on a beautiful hill nearby. The woman still hesitated. He then said to her, "I will personally come down here and take you to your new home before I let my men destroy this one." She agreed to his terms and he went on his way.

Later on that week, construction started in the neighborhood. Everyone on the construction team heard about this woman. As they were busy bringing bulldozers and other equipment into the neighborhood, one man commented that the little old lady in the run-down house was probably terrified they were going to destroy her home with her still inside. The construction worker knocked on her door and assured her they wouldn't do anything to her home until she had moved out. Just then, the elderly woman smiled confidently, and told the man, "Don't be concerned for me, young man. The owner himself told me he'd come down and take me to my new home before he destroyed this old one."

This is a picture of how loving our Lord is. He will not allow the destruction of the world to take place until Jesus comes down and personally brings us to our new home. The rapture is God's love taking us out of this world before He allows this old world to be destroyed.

Chapter 11

The Drawing Power of Grace

Have you ever wondered why it seems that many people do not draw near to God? Have you also ever wondered why some people run to God only as needs arise? In my experience, I have also known many people who truly believed in Jesus, but instead of running to him in times of need, they would run from him; instead of coming to church to build their faith they'd avoid it, and instead of reading the Bible when they needed wisdom and direction, they'd neglect it.

I believe one thing causes people like this to move in a direction away from God, and that is fear: unwarranted fear brought on by wrong concepts concerning God. One of the tools the enemy uses against us is deception. A classic example of Satan's use of deception is during Jesus' temptation in the wilderness. The last words the Father had said to Jesus before that event was when the Holy Spirit had come upon him at baptism. He heard the Father say, "This is My beloved Son, in whom I am well pleased" (Matthew 3:17). Yet as soon as the devil began tempting Jesus during that time in the wilderness, he said, "If you are the Son of God, command that these stones become bread" (Matthew 4:2). The devil always tries to deceive us into thinking God doesn't really love us.

When you know how much someone loves you, it drives out any fear of approaching that person. But when it comes to approaching God, fears can sometimes surface when one faces trials and begins thinking that God is punishing him for his sins.

> *1 John 4:17, 18*
> *"Love has been perfected among us in this: that we may have boldness in the day of judgment; because as He is, so are we in this world. There is no fear in love; but perfect love casts out fear, because fear involves torment. But he who fears has not been made perfect in love."*

Here's the problem with fear: If it is in you, it will always cause you to back away from God. The "perfect love" noted in the above verse is love that comes from God toward us, not our love toward God. John is not saying that if you are practicing perfect love you will drive out all fear in your life. He is saying if we believe in God's love toward us, this perfect love will drive out fear.

> **"Here's the problem with fear: If it is in you, it will always cause you to back away from God."**

When I was younger, my mom and dad would take me and my sister camping. There would be other campers nearby, and sometimes they'd be doing things like washing their dirty dishes in the river. I remember Dad telling me, "You can drink out of the river if people who are washing dishes are way up beyond us because the river purifies itself." I'd never forgotten that. Just like a river that washes away any impurities within it, so will the perfect love of God drive out any forms of fear within us when we choose to run to Him.

Fear of the Lord

There is a common mistake that people make regarding the topic of the fear of the Lord. It is the distinction that must be made before and after the work of the cross. As we discussed in earlier chapters, sins were only covered before the cross, whereas they were completely removed after the cross. Before the sacrifice of Jesus, God's wrath came upon the disobedient, but we must remember that after the cross, God swore He would never pour His wrath on His people again.

Under the Mosaic law, people were so afraid of God that they would tell Moses to go before the Lord on their behalf; they were terrified of His presence. Several times in scripture when people encountered the appearance of God, they thought they would die! Why? Their sins were only covered at that time and they operated under sin consciousness. We can relate to this feeling on a very earthly level. Suppose you were driving around knowing that you had an outstanding parking ticket and you suddenly see a police car behind you with red lights flashing. Your heart races and you only calm down after he's passed you to pull over another driver. Why? Because you know you are guilty and have not paid the consequences for your actions.

Judgment

Even the prophets of the Old Testament were afraid of God to the point of feeling as though they'd be overtaken by death. Isaiah himself, the one who prophesied concerning the coming of Jesus felt this way.

> *Isaiah 6:1-7*
> *"In the year that King Uzziah died, I saw the Lord sitting on a throne, high and lifted up, and the train of His robe filled the temple. Above it stood seraphim; each one had six wings: with two he covered his face, with two he covered his feet, and with two he flew. And one cried to another and said:*
> *"Holy, holy, holy is the Lord of hosts;*
> *The whole earth is full of His glory!"*
> *And the posts of the door were shaken by the voice of him who cried out, and the house was filled with smoke. So I said,*
> *"Woe is me, for I am undone! Because I am a man of unclean lips, and I dwell in the midst of a people of unclean lips; for my eyes have seen the King, the Lord of hosts."*
> *Then one of the seraphim flew to me, having in his hand a live coal which he had taken with the tongs from the altar. And he touched my mouth with it, and said:*
> *"Behold, this has touched your lips; your iniquity is taken away, and your sin purged."*

Isaiah had to be cleansed in order to stand before God because of the sin in his life. This is the wonderful thing about the gospel, for all our sins have been removed and we no longer need to stand in fear of judgment.

There is a difference between standing at the judgment seat of Christ as a believer and as a non-believer. For the believer, it is not a matter of whether or not they are heavenbound, but whether or not they will receive eternal rewards based on their works on earth (1 Corinthians 3:11-15; 2 Thessalonians 1:7).

There is a story in 2 Samuel 6 where God struck one of David's soldiers dead because he had put his hand out to steady the ark as it was being transported. David and his men recovered the ark from the hand of the Philistines and were bringing it back into Jerusalem. When one of the oxen stumbled, a man named Uzzah had taken hold of the ark to stabilize it. But the Lord killed him on the spot for improperly handling it.

I remember years ago watching the first Indiana Jones film, *Raiders of the Lost Ark*, at the movie theater. Near the end, Indiana and his girlfriend are tied to a pole while a German soldier opens up the ark. Indiana tells his girlfriend not to open her eyes. Immediately, a cloud emerges from the ark and kills everyone, but it doesn't touch the two heroes. I recall thinking to myself afterward, *I wonder if I'd be killed if I had touched the ark?* Well, back then I didn't know the things I know now about God's grace. Of course, that was just a movie, but the truth is God's wrath will not come upon those who are His, as that wrath was placed on Jesus on our behalf. There should now no longer be fear in approaching God, my friend, for His love has saved us.

Sin consciousness kept people from approaching God in the Old Testament. They did not want to draw near to Him. Under the law, the high priest was to enter the Holiest of Holies once a year. It was such a fearful thing to do that a rope would be tied around one of the priest's ankles in case he committed some error while inside. The priest would have to be pulled out with the rope because he would have immediately been struck dead by the presence of God for his offense. But let us compare that to now. Now, we as Christians are the temple of God. The Bible tells us this.

I Corinthians 6:19
"...do you not know that your body is the temple of the Holy Spirit who is in you, whom you have from God, and you are not your own?"

The word used for "temple" in the above text is the Greek word *naos*, specifically defined as *a temple, a shrine, that part of the temple where*

God himself resides. This was the portion of the temple where only the high priest could enter. When Jesus died on the cross, the physical veil that separated the holy place from the Holiest of Holies was torn from top to bottom, indicating that there was now access into the presence of God at all times. We have become God's temple, because His Holy Spirit resides within us.

Up Close and Personal

We briefly discussed the following verse early on in Chapter 2, but this bears repeating as we look more closely at what it means to truly behold Christ.

> *2 Corinthians 3:17, 18*
> *"Now the Lord is the Spirit; and where the Spirit of the Lord is, there is liberty. But we all, with unveiled face, beholding as in a mirror the glory of the Lord, are being transformed into the same image from glory to glory, just as by the Spirit of the Lord."*

For years after my salvation experience, I'd attend church and people would tell me that if I desired to change, it was all about me changing my behavior. I made many attempts to do just that, but what the scriptures tell us is exactly the opposite. As I mentioned in the second chapter of this book, it is the presence of the Son that changes us. Think for a moment what the physical sun is capable of doing to you. If you're on vacation in Maui and you come back home with a dark tan, you don't go around telling people how you walked the beach and worked hard all day to get that tan—you simply got it by being exposed to the sun. When we remain exposed to the Son, Jesus, we cannot help but be changed!

This brings me to another point: The act of beholding Jesus must be done "up close and personal." Let's say a mother is preparing to change her baby's clothes. She cannot do it unless she's right in front of that baby; she can't do it from another room in the house. The baby does nothing except look cute while Mom does all the work! My point is that we need to get close to the Lord in order for His glory to change us. Let us take our position before God, look into the perfect law of liberty, and allow it to change us!

Change Should be Lasting

Let me show you one difference between law and grace. Under the law, people tried to change their lives by doing the works of the law, so if they desired to remain changed they had to continue to do the required works. One of the problems with this process, however, is that this didn't require spending any time with God; it didn't require relationship to do the works of the law. Lasting change was not possible under this system because the responsibility was placed upon the one trying to keep the law.

Grace is entirely different. We are changed by spending time with Jesus, so any area of our lives where he changes us is maintained by simply being with him. The gospel of grace promotes lasting change by remaining in fellowship with the Lord. Some of the greatest blessings we can receive from the Lord come as a result of drawing near to him. Elisha was a servant of Elijah the prophet who had a mighty anointing from God. But the Lord called Elijah home. Elisha sensed what was about to take place and had a request for the senior prophet. In 2 Kings 2, Elisha asked to inherit a double portion, or a double anointing. Elijah told him that this was a hard thing to ask, but if he saw him taken away by God, then it would be granted to him. Elisha stayed close to the Father and received his double portion.

If you have been desiring lasting change in your life, yet you find up to this point nothing has really worked, then the question I ask of you is this: How badly do you want it? Do you desire change badly enough that you would choose to remain close to God through every season of your life, or do you allow yourself to drift away?

If you believe you cannot get close to God because of your imperfections, then the more you focus on those flaws, the less you will desire to draw near to Him. If you are truly desiring change, you must get rid of all wrong thinking that keeps God at a distance. Always remember this: The root of all fear is condemnation. Condemnation makes us feel useless, much like a condemned building. Condemned buildings don't have a function, and inside, they are often wrecked. You have got to remember that this is not who you are, and that you are indeed someone who has the right and privilege to go before our King!

In the scriptures, there are many examples of people who possessed great faith, not in their own righteousness, but faith in the righteousness of God. Take, for example, the centurion in Matthew 8. The centurion desired healing for his servant, but told Jesus he was not worthy for him to come into his house, but to only say the word and his servant would be healed. The faith the centurion displayed was faith in the righteousness of Jesus. A few chapters later in Matthew 15, we see the faith of the Canaanite woman who begged Jesus to heal her daughter. She was not a Jew, and Jesus had even alluded to her unrighteousness by using a metaphor, saying that, "It is not good to take the children's bread and throw it to the little dogs." She acknowledged that,"...even little dogs eat the crumbs which fall from the masters' table." She recognized that within her there was no self-righteousness, but she placed her faith in the righteousness of Jesus. This is why Jesus answered her by saying her faith was great.

If you are choosing to draw near to God or are desiring to accomplish anything in faith, you must believe God has given you the gift of righteousness through Jesus. No wonder Jesus prayed so powerfully the night before he was crucified, praying for all believers, "that they may be made perfect in one, and that the world may know that You have sent Me, and have loved them as You have loved Me" (John 17:23).

Jesus himself prayed that you would know that the Father loves you as Jesus is loved. Don't hesitate to draw near to Him.

Chapter 12
Unchanging Love

One of the greatest truths found in the Bible is that God loves us unconditionally. Unconditional love is a decision to love someone whether that person is good or bad. Unconditional love decides that love will not be withheld despite someone's personal performance towards you. God's love toward us is unchanging. He doesn't get up one morning and say, *I'll love them today because they've been pretty good*, and then gets up another morning and says, *Well, I've changed my mind. They came up short doing my perfect will today, so they're undeserving of my affection.*

My wife and I love going to Hawaii for vacation and enjoy visiting the many islands there. Unfortunately, I'd often experience seasickness during those jaunts on the boat. During one trip I was told that if I started feeling nauseous to begin fixing my eyes on a non-moving object, such as the shoreline. I was told that concentrating on a stable object would settle my stomach. In the same way when our faith is wavering, we need to fix our spiritual eyes on the unchanging love of God. If we focus on His unconditional love toward us, we will no longer question His motives regarding us. We need to understand that He will welcome us into His presence and that His arms are open to us at all times. The deeper we are able to grasp His love for us, the more we are going to change, and the greater we will be able to comprehend His incredible love. This revelation allows us to receive freely from Him. The following verse proves that we can know this love that comes from our Heavenly Father.

Ephesians 3:14-21
"For this reason I bow my knees to the Father of our Lord Jesus Christ, from whom the whole family in heaven and earth is named, that He would grant you, according to the riches of His glory, to be strengthened with might through His Spirit in the inner man, that Christ may dwell in your hearts through faith; that you, being rooted and grounded in love, may be able to comprehend with all the saints what is the width and length and depth and height—to know the love of Christ which passes knowledge; that you may be filled with all the fullness of God. Now to Him who is able to do exceedingly abundantly above all that we ask or think, according to the power that works in us, to Him be glory in the church by Christ Jesus to all generations, forever and ever. Amen."

Many people within the church will often stop attending when they are being disobedient in an area of their lives. Many even stop praying, or breaking fellowship with God, for they don't want any reminders of their disobedience to the truth. This is what happened to Adam and Eve in the garden of Eden before the fall of man. Once they died spiritually, they tried hiding from God. But the truth is God does not want us to run *from* Him; instead He desires for us to run *to* Him!

Grieving the Holy Spirit

Let me show you a truth regarding this verse below that will help you see the love of God more clearly.

Ephesians 4:30
"And do not grieve the Holy Spirit of God, by whom you were sealed for the day of redemption."

Many people misinterpret this verse by looking at it through a lens of guilt. What is this verse really saying to us? What does it mean to grieve over someone? Let me give you an example. Let's say you and I were having a conversation and I noticed that you looked really down. I would ask you, "What's going on?" If you responded by saying your father just died, I would have compassion toward you and give you my sympathies, but I would not personally grieve if I didn't know your father. It is only when you love someone that you grieve over them. When a loved one in Christ dies, we may grieve because we can't be with them any longer on this earth, but know in our hearts that our loved one is in heaven. When we sin the Holy Spirit is grieved because he cannot be close to us when we decide to walk in ways contrary to God's will. The very fact that the Holy Spirit can grieve over us reveals God's great love and concern toward His children.

In the garden of Eden before sin existed, Adam and Eve regularly met with God, walking and talking with Him. After Adam and Eve had sinned, they missed that appointed time as they hid away from His presence. What is so significant is that God came and called out to Adam, "Where are you?" (Genesis 3:9). When we read the Bible, it is often difficult to grasp the emotion which an individual felt about a situation when it only records what was said. I personally think God was displeased that Adam and Eve had missed their appointed time to walk with Him in the garden.

My wife and I set aside certain times when we get together and just sit and talk, and I get really upset when she misses that appointment. If I get an emergency call and miss our time together, she can also become disappointed. We both constantly look forward to our times together.

We must remember that God wants to spend time with us. If we have been disobedient toward God, we need to understand that He desires for us to return to Him and that He is willing and able to forgive us. One of my favorite verses in the Bible is Ephesians 3:20 which was highlighted at the beginning of this chapter. It says in part that God is able to do exceedingly above all we ask or think. Most people believe God is able, but question whether He is "willing" and question all kinds of things about what God will and will not do, such as forgive our sin and restore our broken relationship with Him.

> "God cannot deny those who have become part of His body. Once attached, the Lord will never cut you off from himself."

We must discover how much God loves us because once we know, we won't question whether He is willing. He loves us like a parent loves his children. Even when children make mistakes, the parent does not disown them for their shortcomings; a parent loves his children unconditionally, for they are his own. When my kids were teenagers I remember telling them, "Whatever you do in life, I want you to know that your mother and I will always love you unconditionally." This gives a steadiness to a relationship when you know that you can always count on someone and that he or she is always there for you. How much more can we rely on God for His faithfulness?

2 Timothy 2:13
"If we are faithless, He remains faithful; He cannot deny Himself."

Why would Paul say even when we are faithless, Jesus remains faithful and will not deny us? Think about that for a moment. When Peter denied the Lord three times, did Jesus begin to deny that he knew Peter? On the contrary, at his first appearance after his resurrection, Jesus told Mary to go and tell his disciples that he had risen, and specifically, to tell Peter. Jesus went out of his way to reveal to Peter that he would certainly not deny him.

God cannot deny those who have become part of His body. Once attached, the Lord will never cut you off from himself.

John 10:27-30
"My sheep hear My voice, and I know them, and they follow Me. And I give them eternal life, and they shall never perish; neither shall anyone snatch them out of My hand. My Father, who has given them to Me, is greater than all; and no one is able to snatch them out of My Father's hand. I and My Father are one."

Find this verse in your Bible and circle or highlight the words "shall never." It literally means *by no means* or *this will certainly not happen.* It is a double negative in the Greek and it is a phrase used concerning the children of God. You find the same use of it again in John 4:13, when Jesus is speaking to the woman at the well.

John 4:13
"Jesus answered and said to her, 'Whoever drinks of this water will thirst again, but whoever drinks of the water that I shall give him will never thirst. But the water that I shall give him will become in him a

fountain of water springing up into everlasting life.'"

The words "will never" are the same words used in Greek to state a double negative, meaning here that, *if you drink of this (water/eternal life), by no means at all shall you ever thirst again.*

After the fall of Adam, God drove him and Eve out of paradise and placed two angels at the east of Eden to guard the way to the tree of life so that no one could partake of it. At first glance it seems harsh, but God put those angels there because if man had partaken of the tree of life in his fallen state, he would have remained spiritually dead. It was an act of mercy which caused God to guard the tree of life. Thousands of years later, God sent His Son into the world to die for our sins. Once that act was accomplished, eternal life was available to those who would believe. God grants us eternal life because all of our sins are now forgiven—this is how we can now live forever with Him.

Eternal life is much more than just living forever; every spirit being lives forever, but eternal life is to have life with God forever. Let me tell you what it would take for anyone born again to be separated from God after salvation. This means that Jesus himself would have to cut off a part of his body, for we are the body of Christ. When you believed on Christ for salvation, you were given a "one-way ticket" with no return ticket. The Lord Jesus is not going to amputate any part of his body. When you reach heaven, there will be no foreclosure signs on any homes, so to speak. Everyone will have a place. Jesus cannot deny himself. As he is, so are we in this world (1 John 4:17).

Taking the Blinders Off of Love

If we are going to be people who have great faith in God, it is going to come as a result of believing in God's great love for us. One way the devil tries to deceive God's people is by trying to convince them that God does not love them. You see, there are many people in the church who feel like God has somehow given them the "short end of the stick"—that He doesn't really care about their problems or concerns. This way of thinking weakens faith.

From the very beginning, Satan has used this method of deception toward God's people. It began in the garden of Eden.

Genesis 3:1-4

"Now the serpent was more cunning than any beast of the field which the Lord God had made. And he said to the woman, "Has God indeed said, 'You shall not eat of every tree of the garden'?
And the woman said to the serpent, "We may eat the fruit of the trees of the garden; but of the fruit of the tree which is in the midst of the garden, God has said, 'You shall not eat it, nor shall you touch it, lest you die.'

Then the serpent said to the woman, "You will not surely die. For God knows that in the day you eat of it your eyes will be opened, and you will be like God, knowing good and evil."

Satan implied that God didn't love Eve because God was withholding something "good" from her; the devil caused Eve to question whether God really wanted to see her blessed or not.

Think of the people whom you know who no longer attend church because perhaps they think God has been unfair to them, or thought that they were treated unfairly by others. This tactic is Satan's oldest trick: causing people to believe that God is "holding out" on them, or that God truly doesn't love them.

Satan has taken advantage of people for thousands of years with this method. Think of Satan as a conniving man at a woman's place of work. Imagine this woman sharing some personal secrets with this man about her marriage, and the man begins to tell her things like, *I would never treat you badly. If you were mine, I'd really take care of you.* In reality, all this man is thinking of is seducing this woman. He'd say anything she wants to hear, but in the end is only thinking of himself. That's Satan for you.

It's so important that we become established in the love that God really has toward us, especially during those times when we do not understand why things seem to be going wrong. We must learn to trust Him, even during those times in our lives when nothing makes sense. Never doubt His love for you, for if you believe He loves you, it will drive out all doubt and fear from your life, and your faith will soar.

I want you to see that people of faith operate under a different system than the world's system. Once you get a grip on this truth, it will help establish your belief in the love of God.

Colossians 1:12, 13
"...giving thanks to the Father who has qualified us to be partakers of the inheritance of the saints in the light. He has delivered us from the power of darkness and conveyed us into the kingdom of the Son of His love..."

I want you to look at the word conveyed in the scripture above. It can also be translated as "transfer" or "transport." We can read this same scripture as, *He has delivered us from the power of darkness and transferred, or translated us into the kingdom of the Son of His love...* Picturing this reminds me of the TV show **Star Trek**, when Captain Kirk or Mr. Spock is transported from one place to another, they are literally taken out of one environment and placed in another. When you were saved, you were transported out of the system of justice to the system of grace in Christ Jesus.

Final Judgments

Revelation 20:11-14 ESV
"Then I saw a great white throne and him who was seated on it. From his presence earth and sky fled away, and no place was found for them. And I saw the dead, great and small, standing before the throne, and books were opened. Then another book was opened, which is the book of life. And the dead were judged by what was written in the books, according to what they had done. And the sea gave up the dead who were in it, Death and Hades gave up the dead who were in them, and they were judged, each one of them, according to what they had done. Then Death and Hades were thrown into the lake of fire. This is the second death, the lake of fire. anyone's name was not found written in the book of life, he was thrown into the lake of fire."

The Bible shows there are two primary judgments: the great white throne of judgment, which is described in the previous text, and the judgment seat of Christ (2 Corinthians 5:10). Let me explain the judgment at the great white throne. This is the final judgment for those who have died without Christ. The scriptures describe "the dead," which refer to those people who have died without Christ. It says that "the books were opened," which are the books which recorded all that they did, whether good or bad, and then another book was opened called the book of life. The verse then goes on to say that if their names were not found in the book of life, they were cast into the lake of fire.

From a general reading of the verse, it suggests that maybe some of these peoples' names were written in the book of life, but in the Greek the word "if" is written as a first-class sentence, indicating a condition that is assumed to be true. Therefore, where the text says, "if their names were not written…" actually means "*since* their names were not written..." This shows that at this judgment, people are judged out of justice and not out of grace.

Even in a court of law today, the love of God is not what is in operation when pleading mercy before the court. All decisions are made based on merit, and if someone is found guilty and asks for mercy, the judge determines mercy based on the defendant's past. In the kingdom of grace, God gives —not based on anything we do good or bad—but purely on what Jesus did for us on the cross.

This is why no believer will be at the great white throne of judgment. We will stand at the judgment seat of Christ. That judgment seat did not even exist until after resurrection of Christ, for Jesus had to pay the price for our sins before God could translate us out of the system of justice to the system of grace. Both of these seats of judgment are final; you cannot appeal to a higher court, for it is the court of the kingdom of God. The difference is one group of people are judged out of justice, and the other is judged out of grace. This is why at the judgment seat of Christ, no one is cast into hell. Each one's work is evaluated, and if the individual's works were done with right motives, they receive an eternal reward (1 Corinthians 3:13-15). The only thing people could lose at the judgment seat of Christ is reward. Praise God for His grace in our lives! For those who believe on Christ, they are in a position of unconditional love. God will continue to love you no matter what you do. God's love is endless toward those who are found in Christ Jesus.

Two Systems

As we've just read, there is a system for those who reject Christ, and there is a system for those who accept him. We are not being governed by the law of sin and death, but we are being governed by the grace of God in our lives.

Romans 6:14
"For sin shall not have dominion over you, for you are not under law but under grace."

Whenever you find a believer who is not living for the Lord, the problem is that they are thinking like someone who is under the system of the world: the system of justice. They think if they do well they will be blessed, and if they do poorly they will not be blessed. People who think in this manner turn to themselves to gauge performance and trust in themselves for results rather than in Christ; this causes them to be dominated by sin. I call this kind of thinking the "lone wolf" mindset: thinking that causes people to believe they can "go it alone." This refers to actions like Peter's, who had said to Jesus, "Even if all are made to stumble because of You, I will never be made to stumble" (Matthew 26:33). Peter's statement was all about himself, about what he believed HE could do. We promote the sin nature when accomplishments becomes all about us. Recall that Galatians 2:20 tells us, "...it is no longer I who lives, but Christ in me..." Do you see the difference?

When people say, *I can do it without God's help*, they are basically lone wolves. Think about it for a moment: even the Lone Ranger had Tanto with him! If we desire to succeed, we must do everything with Christ; never on our own. We need his leading and help in every circumstance.

Stop Questioning His Love

We must stop questioning God's love for us. Jesus said in John 10:10, "The thief does not come except to steal, and to kill, and to destroy. I have come that they may have life, and that they may have it more abundantly." Thoughts that come into your mind that suggest serving God produces unhappiness must be rejected. To this last statement, I can hear some people saying things like this: *Oh Pastor, if I'm going to become a Christian, I'll have to go without things I love and just go through life being miserable!* I am telling you this is completely untrue! Look at the world of money and fame—something there is missing. What good would it be to have endless amounts of cash and have no one like you, or what good is it to be famous when your personal life is in shambles?

Following Christ is the only way we will experience a fulfilled and eternally fruitful life, the God-kind of life. Whenever people do not believe that God loves them, they will rebel toward Him. This is the reason the scriptures tell parents not to provoke their children to wrath (Ephesians 6:4). Children can grow embittered toward their parents if they do not feel loved by them. God loves us and we must believe this if we are going to have great faith in Him.

I have found this next statement I'm going to make to be true as I have seen this over and over again. People who believe that God truly loves them are more positive than those who think otherwise. I believe those who lack the revelation of God's love tend to find fault with others instead of trying to find the good. 1 Corinthians 13:6, 7 says that love, "...does not rejoice in iniquity, but rejoices in the truth; bears all things, believes all things, hopes all things, endures all things."

Years ago, I heard about an experiment that was conducted on two children. Apparently, a study was being done on how circumstances or environments affected pessimistic and optimistic kids. The pessimistic child was taken into a room full of toys. The boy inspected each toy before glumly stating that the one he wanted was not in the room. The second boy, the optimistic one, was brought into a room that had nothing but horse manure in it. He looked around and exclaimed that there must be a pony around somewhere! The outcome was clear: The positive child was expecting an outcome of good; the negative child could only find what was wrong.

Changing Sides in a Trial

Here's what can happen to some people when they face some kind of trial or a time of testing: Pressure and hardship cause some to "switch sides" and move over to the enemy's camp instead of staying on the right side of love. I know this to be true. I want to take a moment to minister directly to some of you that are reading these words right now. Maybe you've been injured during a trial and you "changed sides." Perhaps you've blamed God for unfair treatment. That attitude of blame can hinder your faith from believing God for the miracles you need in life. The best thing to do is go to God and let Him heal your heart, for He still loves you even if you're angry at him. God's love is unconditional; it does not waver and it does not change toward you.

Figuratively speaking, trials will either cause us to look for the pony when we see the manure, or it will keep us dissatisfied even when there truly is good to be found. Let's begin to expect good from God, no matter what the situation looks like. If you have found yourself on the wrong side while facing a trial and you want to begin operating in the love of God, then understanding that you are loved is so important if you are going to repent for wrong actions.

Luke 15:4-7
"What man of you, having a hundred sheep, if he loses one of them, does not leave the ninety-nine in the wilderness, and go after the one which is lost until he finds it? And when he has found it, he lays it on his shoulders, rejoicing. And when he comes home, he calls together his friends and neighbors, saying to them, 'Rejoice with me, for I have found my sheep which was lost!' I say to you that likewise there will be more joy in heaven over one sinner who repents than over ninety-nine just persons who need no repentance."

We know that this is a parable Jesus told comparing lost sheep to those who repent and return to God. But what I want to ask you is this: what did the lost sheep do in order to be found? He did nothing except trust in the shepherd as he picked him up and returned him to the flock. Let's imagine this sheep's story in a little more detail. Let's say that before this sheep became lost, he was just hanging out with his pals munching on some grass but for some reason, decided to break away from the flock. Maybe he became distracted or was focusing on something in the distance that caused him to lose his way. Now, this little sheep is alone and possibly in great danger. He doesn't know what else to do other than try to hide as things around him become darker and darker as night approaches. Suddenly, he hears the familiar voice of the shepherd calling! He sees the smiling shepherd as he reaches for him and gently lifts him over his shoulder. The sheep doesn't struggle to get free or attempt to run back home on his own; he lets the shepherd carry him because he trusts the shepherd.

In the parable, the emphasis is placed on how the shepherd feels when he finds his lost sheep. He rejoices and tells his friends how wonderful it is that his sheep was found. This shows us how much God loves to welcome back those who have been away from him. For years I'd heard that when someone gets saved, the angels rejoice in heaven, but look carefully at what is actually written just a few verses later in Luke 15:10. The scripture reads, "Likewise, I say to you, there is joy <u>in the presence of the angels</u> of God over one sinner who repents" (underline added). God Himself is the one who is in the midst of the angels rejoicing for the one who has returned. Praise God for His unending love!

Chapter 13
The Hidden Ingredient of Grace

It had been a long, hard year. I was preaching and teaching a lot in our church as usual, but I had also been studying voraciously on the topic of grace. I had been studying this topic intensely for several years, and the more I studied, the more excited I became as I rediscovered foundations of truth which I had studied years and years earlier. As a younger Christian, I had studied and listened to many wonderful preachers. Grace was a newly found truth to me at that time—and I often found myself studying late into the night and then preaching about what the Holy Spirit was opening up to me. It was such a refreshing time for me personally, and through that period we saw a great move of God within our church. Love had been released mightily and was changing lives.

One Saturday evening I had been studying and listening to different messages on the topic, and when I wrapped up my studies that night, I asked myself, *What have I learned?* I concluded, *It doesn't really matter what I do; what really matters is what I believe.* Just then, the Lord said something to me: "If you really believe, then you will act." It was like a rushing, mighty wave of revelation that hit me, and I began to understand things about the concept of belief that I had never seen before.

I began realizing that many people within the modern church do not believe that "believing" requires anything but saying it. My friend, if believing only requires words out of our mouths, then why did Jesus say in Matthew 7:21, "Not everyone who says to Me, 'Lord, Lord,' shall enter the kingdom of heaven, but he who does the will of My Father in heaven"? Jesus was expressing they were saying all the right things, but they had not really responded to the things they were saying.

The repetition of the title "Lord, Lord" used in the verse above was a typical way that people of that time expressed a deep love for someone. Use of a repeated name conveyed great emotion. Another example would be found in Luke 10:41 where Jesus consoled Martha about her concerns. He said to her, "Martha, Martha, you are worried about many things." Also, Jesus, as he hung on the cross in utter anguish said, "My God, My God." In the Old Testament when David learned that his son was killed, he repeatedly cried out, "O my son Absalom—my son, my son Absalom!" As you can see, according to Matthew 7:21 those who would cry out, "Lord, Lord" thought that they had a close relationship with God. The Word can be easily spoken, but when one really believes, it will manifest itself through deeds. I am seeing within the church today that many are confused as to why they are not receiving from God when they say they are believing for their various needs. It's because there is a "hidden ingredient" to grace which people often do not detect, and it's robbing them of what God has called them to personally receive.

> **"The Word can be easily spoken, but when one really believes, it will manifest itself through deeds."**

Many have not dared to go where I am taking you right now for fear of being put under the law or being called a legalist, but as you read this, I believe revelation will come and you will see what real faith looks like and how real faith responds. There is a reason why, in churches today, there is very little spoken about repentance, and very little is spoken concerning judgment. It is because there is an improper view of the gospel of grace. I believe when you see the whole counsel of God, it will give you grit and stamina and the ability to prevail over any circumstances in your life.

Now, I'll be the first to say that I do not know everything in the Word;

all I can do is show you what God has been revealing to me, and ask you to examine what I'm teaching and weigh it against the scriptures. If the Word confirms what I'm saying, then make it part of your life. My desire is to help the church become the mighty force God has intended for it to be in the world.

Good Questions to Ask

I think it would be a good thing to ask yourself a few questions as you continue through this book. Ask yourself, *Am I doing less of the Word than I did in the beginning, when I was new to the faith?* Be honest as you ask yourself, *Am I as hungry for God as I once was? Have I lowered my standards over the years in following Him?* If you answered YES to any of these questions, you may be missing that hidden ingredient and you need to add it into your faith so it can be fruitful and abound for the Lord throughout your lifetime.

Repentance is spoken about so very rarely from the pulpit nowadays. Why does it seem that so many churches today no longer have altar calls? Could it be that it's because we have redefined repentance in a way which no longer points in the right direction? What I believe has happened is that our attempts to understand grace have skewed our views on repentance. We define grace as being "undeserved or unmerited favor" and that is true. We have also boldly proclaimed that we are not saved by our works, therefore nothing we do can save us, and that is true. But if we assume that no change needs to take place, then this is the area where we must readjust our thinking.

I believe we have taken the definition of grace and allowed it to redefine what repentance is. We have said that repentance simply means to *change the mind,* and while that is true, it also means *to turn.* The Greek word for repentance is made from two words: *meta,* meaning *after*; and *noeo,* which means *to perceive.* One of the best ways to understand what a word means in the Bible is to see how it is used. The word "repentance" in the Bible is always used in context of someone turning to God as they turn away from their sinful life. True repentance is a 180° turn. If you have truly changed your mind, then you will truly change direction in life.

Acts 9:35
"So all who dwelt at Lydda and Sharon saw him and <u>turned to the</u>

Lord."

Acts 11:21
"And the hand of the Lord was with them, and a great number believed and underlined to the Lord."

1 Thessalonians 1:9
"For they themselves declare concerning us what manner of entry we had to you, and how you <u>turned to God from idols to serve the living and true God,</u>" (underline emphasis added)

Repenting doesn't mean you are going to stop sinning on your own. It means you will turn to God for help, and it is His help which enables you to quit sinning. Repentance is not an end in and of itself; it is the path that leads to God's help.

Let's look at the opposite of repentance. In Acts 7, Stephen addresses the high priests and eloquently conveys the entire story of the Jews up until the time of Christ's crucifixion. Stephen says this about the Israelites rebelling against God:

Acts 7:38, 39
"This is he who was in the congregation in the wilderness with the Angel who spoke to him on Mount Sinai, and with our fathers, the one who received the living oracles to give to us, whom our fathers would not obey, but rejected. And in their hearts they turned back to Egypt…"

The scriptures say that the Israelites "turned back to Egypt" by rejecting and disobeying God. Being unrepentant is all about turning back to the old way of life or turning back to living a life that is displeasing to the Lord. We want to be headed in the direction that turns toward Him, not in the direction that faces the world.

Fruits Worthy of Repentance

As John the Baptist began his ministry, preparing the way for hearts to receive the truth concerning Jesus, he would speak to those who would venture to hear him in the wilderness. The Bible says in Matthew 3 that those in Jerusalem, Judea, and those in the region of Jerusalem all came out to hear him and to be baptized in the Jordan River. The teachers of the law, the Pharisees and the Sadducees, also came out to hear John. But note what John said to them.

> *Matthew 3:8*
> *"Who warned you to flee from the wrath to come? Therefore bear fruits worthy of repentance…"*

John the Baptist did not just tell the teachers of the law to repent, but to bear fruits worthy of repentance. Fruits of repentance are different than the act of repentance itself. For example, an apple tree has apples, but you wouldn't call an apple a tree any more than you'd call a tree an apple. Fruits of repentance grow out of a changed life, but repentance itself is simply the avenue by which change can begin to take place. If we don't truly desire to turn from a sinful lifestyle, then we are not displaying true repentance. Repentance always involves turning away from the things which are displeasing to God and then turning to Him and His ways. The truth of the matter is one cannot really be saved without this kind of repentance.

Think of repentance in this way: It's like being rescued from a sinking ship. The rescue helicopter is hovering over you and a man from the helicopter is being lowered down. He shouts that you must let go of the ship's railing in order for him to grab hold of you. At that point you have a choice—either turn toward your help and release the railing or remain clutching onto the sinking ship and go down to the depths with it.

When we believe upon the Lord, it doesn't happen because we decided to get "cleaned up" first. It simply means that we turn from our own ways toward Christ. Jesus cleanses us of our sin, but our part is in the turning away from the world and facing God.

Repenting of Unbelief

I am deeply concerned about people who have a mental ascent towards God, but not a real act of repentance operating in their lives. If we understand repentance, we will be able to successfully repent of unbelief. The way to repent of unbelief is by turning away from ideas and concepts which attempt to convince us that God is not who He says He is, and instead choosing to believe God's Word over man's ideas. In Hebrews 3:19, it says that the Israelites wandered in the wilderness for 40 years and could not enter the promised land because of their unbelief. In the next chapter of Hebrews, verse 11 admonishes the church to, "Let us therefore be diligent to enter that rest, lest anyone fall according to the same example of disobedience." The writer of Hebrews concludes that unbelief is in fact disobedience.

Israel would not obey God because they would not turn away from Egypt, but instead kept looking back and desiring to return to the same life they had before. Therefore, when the Bible states that the Israelites would not mix their faith with the promises of God, it simply means that they refused to turn away from "the world," in their case, their longing for Egypt. This cost them entrance into the promised land. It was not just a matter of their need to change their mind; they had to change direction in order to follow God. In the same way, if we are going to follow God, we not only change our minds from previous thinking, but we change direction as well.

Successful Counseling

I used to do a lot of marriage counseling in our church. Before counseling couples, I had two requirements that must first be met: the first was that the couples would agree to attend services, and the second was that they would agree to employ my counsel as long as it was backed up scripturally. I found that nine out of ten couples would return to me after a service and explain that they knew what they were to do because God had revealed it to them. His presence gave them clear direction on what to do. I personally believe a lot of counseling is fruitless because the act of repentance is not a requirement. Simply listening and doing the same old "song and dance" for years concerning problems does not move people into a proper direction.

In the apostle Paul's day, there was a man in the church of Corinth who was sleeping with his stepmother, and Paul was appalled at that sin. He had even told the church members to, "deliver such a one to Satan for the destruction of the flesh, that his spirit may be saved in the day of the Lord Jesus" (1 Corinthians 5:5). After the church proceeded to obey, this man eventually repented and we read a powerful statement concerning repentance given to us by the Holy Spirit.

2 Corinthians 7:10
"For godly sorrow produces repentance leading to salvation, not to be

regretted; but the sorrow of the world produces death."

As long as you still want to sin, you will never repent in your life. You have got to get to the point where you just do not want to sin anymore; this is what the Bible calls godly sorrow. Worldly sorrow is different. You feel bad because of the consequences, but you don't feel bad about what you did; only that you got caught and now a penalty must be paid. We can liken this concept to getting a speeding ticket—you usually don't actually feel bad for driving fast, but you feel bad because of the fine you are now obligated to pay.

I want to again take a moment to minister to some of you reading this right now. If you are living with a certain sin that keeps you from receiving God's best, then you must get to the point where you will no longer tolerate it in your life. You must come to the realization that it is not truly fulfilling and is certainly not making your joy full. If you do not reach that point, you will never be able to successfully repent of anything; just being afraid of getting caught is not true repentance. There is a much better way to live when you realize that you cannot be fulfilled unless you commit your way to God and decide to move in His direction.

Sin Never Brings Real Joy

Sin can never bring real happiness in life. It is a counterfeit substance of the real thing. It's like the difference between eating real crab in your salad and eating fake crab; the fake stuff tastes okay but there's no comparison to the real thing! The world tempts us and tries to tell us that we won't be happy unless we do things their way. Drugs are offered; sex outside of marriage is the norm for the world's standards. Those things are all counterfeit representations of the real joy and satisfaction that Jesus offers us. The Bible offers true joy. I love Ephesians 5:18 which tells us, "...do not be drunk with wine, in which is dissipation; but be filled with the Spirit..."

That brings me to a story I want to tell you. I remember after I got saved, I told all my friends that I used to run around with that I got a better "high" than they all got. They asked me what I meant by that. I told them that I got "high" off of Jesus! I remember telling them that it's great to be with Jesus; there's no hangover in the morning, and there are no regrets, and that he gives me joy unspeakable, full of glory! Of course, they thought I was nuts, but that was because they had been deceived into thinking the world had the real thing—that joy unspeakable—when in fact it did not.

Counting the Cost

I want to show you something which seems to conflict with other scriptures, but in fact does not. It deals with something that is free, yet we are told to "count the cost."

Isaiah 55:1
"Ho! Everyone who thirsts,
Come to the waters;
And you who have no money,
Come, buy and eat.
Yes, come, buy wine and milk
Without money and without price."

The verse above is speaking of salvation and that it is free. If that is true then why did Jesus say that we must count the cost of it?

Luke 14:28, 29
"For which of you, intending to build a tower, does not sit down first and count the cost, whether he has enough to finish it—lest, after he has laid the foundation, and is not able to finish, all who see it begin to mock him, saying, 'This man began to build and was not able to finish'?"

What is interesting here is that Jesus says we must count the cost to follow him. But the questions I want to ask you are these: Are you paying a price for the gift of righteousness? Are you paying a price for holiness? What about your position in Christ? To these, the answer is a resounding NO. Before you ever did one thing, Jesus had ascended on high, and was then seated in authority. When you believed on him for your salvation, you also sat down with him in a position of authority, and you hadn't yet done anything good nor bad, so all of your right standing was paid in full.

So, what is the cost about which Jesus is speaking? He is talking about the cost it takes to use your faith. In Jesus' illustration in Luke 14, he says that someone started a building and was not able to finish it; he did not say it was someone who bought a house and then moved into it, and then later was not able to make the payment on it with the bank foreclosing on him. Jesus is talking about a building which has not yet been completed. When you begin believing God for things in your life, those things are not yet manifest, so it takes using your faith on a daily basis to be able to see them to completion. Whether it is using your faith in raising your children until they are grown, or using your faith on an illness until it is completely gone, or using your faith on a loved one until they finally give their life to Christ—it takes faith to see these victories manifest.

The scriptures that tell us "to count the cost" is about the price of believing in faith. It will cost you something to turn to God in repentance. It costs self-control; it costs the denial of fleshly things; it costs time and focus when there is a sincere desire to put faith at work in everyday life.

I could not possibly mention all the times when, during my own personal trials, I felt like saying something negative, yet refused to give life to those words by speaking them. I couldn't count how many times negative thoughts have come to mind, yet rejected their attempts to root into my thinking. True repentance is continually turning to God for help in situations like these and more. If you live in this way you will truly be blessed.

Chapter 14
Responding to His Presence and His Word

There is a big difference between response and reaction. When we react to a situation, a person, or a circumstance, there's no time for thought—only action. Response is different. We take time and ponder; we weigh outcomes, consider possibilities. There is a lot more effort in creating a response.

This is what is so powerful about the gospel of grace. We are given the opportunity to respond to God's great love toward us, and that is what changes our lives forever. Now what I say next may sound controversial to you, but hear me out first. I personally do not believe the most important thing you can do in a church service is to praise God or even to hear the Word, although both are vital and absolutely necessary for a successful Christian life. I believe the most important thing one can do during a church service has to do with responding to God's presence during that time. When all is said and done, the most important thing we can do in response to God's great love for us is to yield to His Spirit.

I'm afraid that over the years in the American church, we have largely embraced entertainment rather than relationship, and we have focused on performance rather than intimacy with God. Intimacy in our relationship with God is just as important—if not more important—as intimacy in a marriage. Could you imagine being married to your spouse and the only real connection you share is a love of movies? Sure, it's fun to watch movies together and maybe discuss them, but that isn't enough depth to sustain a marriage. In the same way, we must cultivate our relationship with God through intimacy.

Hebrews 3:15
"Today, if you will hear His voice,
Do not harden your hearts as in the rebellion."

Hardness of heart comes by repeatedly remaining unresponsive to the Spirit of God. The more one lacks in his or her response to Him, the harder the heart becomes until a day arrives when compromise is fully accomplished. Things that person would have never said or done under the influence of the Holy Spirit are now the norm.

Have you ever been indifferent to truth you have heard, or had taken on the attitude that it really didn't matter that much, because after all, you're living the best way you know how? The Lord comforts and warns us; He gives us guidance, but if we refuse to respond to those times of correction, we lose the opportunity to get on the right path which brings joy and peace. I remember years ago I was preaching during a service, and the Holy Spirit fell on me, and I began to speak prophetically, addressing preachers. I began saying things like, "You need to repent today or something worse is going to happen to you," and I went on and on. At that time, I had no idea a dear friend of mine in ministry was in sin. I was also unaware that only a few weeks later that particular sin would come to light and he would lose everything he had worked for all those years. It was one of the most painful experiences of my life, seeing his family suffer and all of the collateral damage it had caused to those who looked up to him. If only he would have responded to the warning of the Spirit that night, all could have been avoided.

We need to understand that God knows everything about us. He knows what will cause us to fall, and He knows what direction will bring the most peace, but we must respond to His leading. After the incident where Peter denied the Lord three times, and the Lord was in the process of restoring Peter after the resurrection, Jesus asked him three times whether Peter loved him or not. Jesus had told Peter three times to feed his sheep. After the third time of asking Peter the same question, he became grieved. He told the Lord that he knew all things. Peter understood that God knew him better than anyone —what kind of person he was, and how much Peter truly loved him. In the same way, God knows what we can withstand and what we cannot bear, but we must respond to what He is doing in our hearts in order to remain on the proper path.

God Sends Us Clear Messages

When I first started out in ministry, I had a particularly sobering experience. I was studying for the ministry and was working a regular job during the day. During the evenings I'd work on a correspondence course. One Wednesday night I had said to the Lord, *Maybe I should stay home on Wednesdays and study.* I hadn't heard the Lord's response to what I was contemplating and prepared to go to church that night with my family. After the message that evening, my pastor approached me and told me he wanted me to meet a friend who operated in the gift of words of knowledge. I shook hands with him and he instantly stopped and said, "If you leave the sheepfold, the wolf will kill you." Needless to say, I got that personal message loud and clear.

I'm not suggesting we obey everything people say to us, but when the Holy Spirit is bearing witness with our own hearts, we must respond to God by obeying His directions. I wonder how my life would have turned out if I had not responded properly to what the Spirit was directing me to do personally. Now please hear me, I am not saying everyone needs to go to every church service in their home church; what I am saying, however, is that the Holy Spirit knows what each person needs and what they don't need. I wonder how many misfortunes and tragedies can be avoided if we simply respond to what God is doing in our hearts? God knows us better than anyone, and He desires to constantly guide us throughout our lives. Some may believe that God does not personally communicate with us, but I don't believe that God has shut down His radio signals; I think sometimes we change frequencies and refuse to listen to His channel.

Secret Seasons

God navigates us through different seasons at various times in life. There are certain times when He guides us and times when He warns us. If we don't know how to properly gauge these seasons through which God desires to take us, we can miss out on what God has planned from before we were even born.

Psalms 1:3
"He shall be like a tree
Planted by the rivers of water,
That brings forth its fruit in its season,
Whose leaf also shall not wither;
And whatever he does shall prosper."

Acts 1:7
"And He said to them, 'It is not for you to know times or seasons which the Father has put in His own authority.'"

If a farmer doesn't sow seeds during the proper season, he will be unable to reap the benefits come harvestime. If he's sowing seeds in the winter that are meant to be sown in the fall, he won't be enjoying his crop in the spring. Likewise, God has appointed certain seasons spiritually where we need to "sow" before we reap the rewards of that season. My point in this is to say that God is fully aware of the right times to speak to you and He knows if you're not open to Him when He speaks, it could cost you a future harvest, spiritually speaking. This is just one reason why it is important to be open at all times to God.

Isaiah 55:6
"Seek the Lord while He may be found; call upon Him when He is near."

God is always near to us, and He will never leave us nor forsake us because of Jesus' sacrifice. But there are times when He reveals Himself in a special way in order to specifically guide and direct us. His manifested presence is not a common occurrence, so do not draw away from Him when He is revealing Himself to you. During those times when you sense His nearness, tell Him, for instance, that you will wake up in the middle of the night to pray, or to remain at the altar even if service has already ended. Just do what you hear the Holy Spirit leading you to do.

It was many years ago when I first experienced the presence of God in this way. I had been in ministry already for many years and my heart just wasn't as soft as it used to be. In some ways, I had grown calloused in my attitude. My wife, Joyce, suggested that we attend a Holy Spirit conference and I agreed to go. Upon our arrival, we received the conference schedule and order of services. The first thing I did was complain to Joyce that the meetings were five hours long. I protested about everything! To tell you the truth, all I wanted to do was head to the meetings late and leave early. I just wanted to go back to our hotel room and watch TV.

We arrived to the first meeting and sat in the back. Even though I entered with a harsh attitude, by the conclusion of the evening I was changed because the presence of God fell upon the meeting so strongly. I felt like it was rain from heaven, refreshing me. I just fell apart in God's presence. Each service after that we began moving our way up until finally we were sitting right up front. As the preacher was speaking during one of the services, the Holy Spirit spoke to me, telling me that the preacher was going to stop and pray for ministers, and that I was to go forward. I wrote down the Holy Spirit's message to me right away and placed it under my seat. Suddenly, the preacher stopped in the middle of his message and said, "The Lord wants me to pray for ministers right now." I immediately ran up to the altar, and before I could even get to the minister, the power of God hit me so hard, it knocked me back and I had to be carried off the stage. I sat for the longest time weeping before the Lord. That incident affected me and my wife for the next six months. Our church was totally consumed and changed by what had taken place, with me being able to bring that love back and share with the entire congregation. That experience transformed me more than any other experience I've ever had since my conversion.

The way we respond to God will either transform us, or it will harden us. I wonder how many times God has visited His people in a service, and they remain indifferent to Him? Perhaps some people think that they are just not really ready to change, so they put off the leading of the Spirit. I believe that you don't want to miss a season of breakthrough, so it's important to learn how to respond to the Holy Spirit if you desire to truly be fruitful throughout your life. Revealing these secrets of grace is like turning a flashlight on in a dark room—once the light is on, we still need to point it in the direction we need to go. I hope you are getting the point that operating in grace does not happen automatically; we must respond to the truth we receive. We must respond to the leading of the Holy Spirit. We must respond to desires He puts within our hearts. Most importantly, we must respond in love.

Romans 6:14 says, "For sin shall not have dominion over you, for you are not under law but under grace." So, if we say we believe correctly and do not believe (or think) like someone under the law, then sin will automatically no longer have dominion over us. But many forget to read the preceding verses which lead to the result of this type of victorious living.

> *Romans 6:12,13*
> *"Therefore do not let sin reign in your mortal body, that you should obey it in its lusts. And do not present your members as instruments of unrighteousness to sin, but present yourselves to God as being alive from the dead, and your members as instruments of righteousness to God."*

Paul is saying here that we need to do something in order to receive these results. Dominion over sin doesn't just automatically "turn on" the way a phone lights up when someone calls. It takes the action of responding correctly in order to receive the results God wants us to have in our lives. The act of believing is wonderful, but when you really believe, you are going to act upon that belief. You have got to do something with your faith!

Too Little Too Late

If Jesus heals then why aren't more people being healed in the church? If Jesus provides then how is it that some within the church don't seem to have proper provision? If God helps restore relationships, then why do so many marriages in the church end in divorce? I know these are hard questions, but I believe part of the problem is that there is "too little too late" when it comes to really responding to what people within the church say they believe. If we are being completely honest, I think all of us over the years have wondered why so many within the church do not seem to receive what God promises. It could very well be a case of too little too late. Some simply wait too long to begin applying the principles of belief in their lives. It is one thing to say we have faith; it is something else to move upon that faith.

I have noticed over the last few years there seems to be an increase in people falling away from the church—all the way from the pew to the pulpit. I inquired the Lord about this one day, and He said to me, "There is only one reason why this happens." As I listened to the Lord, He proceeded to tell me it was because many hear and do not obey. He then went on to say that if people hear and obey, they will never fall. As soon as He communicated this to me, I recalled what the apostle Peter had said.

1 Peter 1:5-10
"...giving all diligence, add to your faith virtue, to virtue knowledge, to knowledge self-control, to self-control perseverance, to perseverance godliness, to godliness brotherly kindness, and to brotherly kindness love. For if these things are yours and abound, you will be neither barren nor unfruitful in the knowledge of our Lord Jesus Christ. For he who lacks these things is shortsighted, even to blindness, and has forgotten that he was cleansed from his old sins. Therefore, brethren, be even more diligent to make your call and election sure, for if you do these things you will never stumble . . . "

Years ago, I had a preacher friend who I used to joke around with a lot. I'd say to him, "Are you sure you're saved?" And he'd laugh and answer, "We really won't know until the end." Of course, he was kidding, but I believe if you are truly saved you are going to produce good fruit in your life and you will know it.

Matthew 7:21-26
"Not everyone who says to Me, 'Lord, Lord,' shall enter the kingdom of heaven, but he who does the will of My Father in heaven. Many will say to Me in that day, 'Lord, Lord, have we not prophesied in Your name, cast out demons in Your name, and done many wonders in Your name?' And then I will declare to them, 'I never knew you; depart from Me, you who practice lawlessness!'

Therefore whoever hears these sayings of Mine, and does them, I will liken him to a wise man who built his house on the rock: and the rain descended, the floods came, and the winds blew and beat on that house; and it did not fall, for it was founded on the rock.

But everyone who hears these sayings of Mine, and does not do them, will be like a foolish man who built his house on the sand: and the rain descended, the floods came, and the winds blew and beat on that house;

and it fell. And great was its fall."

This teaching from Jesus shows the concept of "too little too late". Here were people who gave the appearance of true believers, but lacked doing the Word in their private lives. In verse 21, take careful note of the word 'says' that Jesus used. It is a participle in the Greek (a verbal adjective) which indicates a continual action. If we liken this story to today, here we see people in the church who are well versed in "Christian talk" *(Praise the Lord, Jesus is good, Amen, and so forth)*. They may say all the right things, but they do not practice the Word. To those types of people, Jesus says, "I don't know you." I think it is worth noting that in the first part of the scripture above, Jesus talks about those who say and do, but in the next paragraph regarding those who build their house on the rock, he talks about those who hear and do. It appears that Jesus is making a point that if we are truly his followers, then we should be able to prove it by our actions. I am fully aware we our not saved by our works—just as we have been exploring throughout this book—but I am equally aware that if we have living faith, it will do more than simply come from our mouths. It will display itself through changed lives.

Belief Reveals Itself

Have you ever heard the expression, *If it looks like a duck and quacks like a duck, then it must be a duck*? We can apply this idea to belief as well. There are those who say, *You don't have to do anything to be saved. All you have to do is believe in what Jesus did.* While that is completely true, there is something for which we are responsible if we are to receive the full benefit of our faith. We don't want to be slack in our response to Him so that we turn out to see "too little too late" in effect.

Now, let's talk about the thief on the cross who died next to Jesus. He certainly didn't have time to do anything! Or did he? Think about it—he actually did do something immediately with his faith by rebuking the other thief. He also did something else by turning to Jesus and asking him to remember him in paradise. Even within our own services at church, when some responds to the altar call, they immediately get up and walk the aisle before confessing Jesus as Lord in their life. That is an action that accompanies belief.

Romans 4:5, 6
"But to him who does not work but believes on Him who justifies the ungodly, his faith is accounted for righteousness, just as David also describes the blessedness of the man to whom God imputes righteousness apart from works..."

Some misunderstand this scripture to mean that those who believe on Christ don't have to do anything at all. No, no, a thousand times no—this would not be an accurate interpretation of the scripture. Paul is talking about the works of the law which were designed to justify those long before Jesus came to be the sacrifice for all. Works of faith do not justify a person, they simply release the benefits of faith.

Throughout this entire book, we've discussed that a person is not saved by their good works. People don't have to go out and feed the poor before they get saved; the don't have to go out and right every wrong they did before coming to Christ. But those types of actions accompany those who believe once they are saved. Here is the truth of the matter: We desire to do good works because we are saved, not to be saved. Just like a bird that hatches out of an egg, it begins immediately acting like a bird. Once a dolphin is birthed, it can't help but act like a dolphin. In the same way, once you are born again, you begin acting like the righteousness of God.

James 1:22
"But be doers of the word, and not hearers only, deceiving yourselves."

The word "hearer" is *akroatés* in the Greek and describes someone who would sit in a classroom yet not do any of the work; someone who's simply auditing the class, but not getting any credit for it. I am concerned that we have too many attending church with this type of mentality, coming in to "audit" and not get any "credit." That would be like getting a gym membership and going every week to look at the equipment but never getting on one of the machines. That would be silly, right? Well, we have got to do more than just hear but do the Word in order to truly release the blessing in our lives.

James 2:20-23
"But do you want to know, O foolish man, that faith without works is dead? Was not Abraham our father justified by works when he offered

Isaac his son on the altar? Do you see that faith was working together with his works, and by works faith was made perfect? And the Scripture was fulfilled which says, "Abraham believed God, and it was accounted to him for righteousness." And he was called the friend of God."

James uses a quote taken from Genesis 15:6 which states that God accounted Abraham as righteous through his belief. That incident occurred 25 years prior to Abraham willingly offering up his son Isaac to the Lord, but this does not mean that Abraham's faith was dead or inactive for 25 years. On the contrary, it was still operating. If you study the life of Abraham you would read that he was constantly displaying his faith. In the opening of chapter 26 of Genesis, the Lord appeared to Isaac, telling him not to consult with King Abimelech of the Philistines, for aid during a famine. Instead, God made a promise to Isaac according to His promise with Abraham, ". . . because Abraham obeyed My voice and kept My charge, My commandments, My statutes, and My laws" (Genesis 26:5). Clearly, Abraham's faith was constantly displaying actions. Going back to Abraham's life years earlier when he offered Isaac up to the Lord, I believe this was the greatest test of faith in which he willingly put his most treasured possession before God.

I believe we can lead others astray if we give the impression that we fully believe and trust in the Lord, yet remain unchanged in our lives. This sort of falsehood gives the impression that faith is alive and working by mere proclamation, while requiring no corresponding action.

There's a true story of a man who walked over Niagara Falls on a tightrope. After he had crossed over to the other side and made his way back, he yelled over the applauding crowd, "How many believe I can go across pushing a wheelbarrow with a man in it?" To which the crowd positively responded. The tightrope walker then proceeded to ask, "Which one of you are going to be that man?" The crowd instantly became silent. With regard to our faith, could it be that we have uttered the words, *I believe*, yet we've not been willing to get in the wheelbarrow? When it comes down to it, faith acts when faith is released. It does not just sit there, and if it does, then it's only for a short period of time.

Let me speak to some of you very intimately right now: If you are not willing to repent—now—you have a faith problem and you are lacking the substance of faith in your life. See, whenever someone falls into sin, it is from a lack of faith. Let me explain. When a husband is unfaithful to his wife, it's because he's trying to find happiness through his own efforts. When someone steals, it's because he's trying to take care of himself apart from God's ways, but when you have faith you look to God to help you find fulfillment. When you have faith, you look to God to be the source of provision in your life.

Works of the Flesh vs. Spirit

We want to be active in believing the Word of God. Not only is it important to a successful Christian life, but we are promised something of the greatest value when we do. Let's examine the other spectrum of belief, which involves the works of the flesh.

> *Galatians 5:19-21*
> *"Now the works of the flesh are evident, which are: adultery, fornication, uncleanness, lewdness, idolatry, sorcery, hatred, contentions, jealousies, outbursts of wrath, selfish ambitions, dissensions, heresies, envy, murders, drunkenness, revelries, and the like; of which I tell you beforehand, just as I also told you in time past, that those who practice such things will not inherit the kingdom of God."*

It seems that Paul is stern in reiterating his point by saying, *I have told you this before. Now I'm going to tell you again. People who do these deeds are not going to get to heaven.* Some have tried to dilute Paul's statement by saying that he's not talking about eternal life—that he's only talking about the blessings of the kingdom. That is a far stretch from what the verse actually says.

It is possible to do something but not believe in it, but it is totally impossible to believe something and not act on it. For instance, if you're married and your spouse gives you vitamins to take every day, you may not believe they'll make a difference in your health, but you go on taking them anyway just to be appeasing. If you enjoy driving fast, you may not believe you need to heed the 55 mile-an-hour freeway speed limit either, but if you see a police officer ahead of you, chances are you'll decrease your speed to the legal limit. This just proves that we do things all the time we don't necessarily believe in. On the other hand, it is not possible to believe in something without actions that correspond to those beliefs. How could I honestly tell my wife and kids I love them yet never show it?

It's impossible. If I love them, I'll undoubtedly display the truth through my actions. Let's look at a scripture that confirms what we do speaks louder than what we say.

> *1 John 3:18*
> *"My little children, let us not love in word or in tongue, but in deed and in truth."*

The apostle John mentions to show love in deed and truth. This is especially important in the day in which we live because what the world defines as "love," the scriptures define differently. For example, we call it "love" to support people who refuse to work when the Bible clearly states that if one will not work he shall not eat (2 Thessalonians 3:10). We see young people living in the basements of their parent's homes who refuse to work, with parents spending their retirement money to provide for them. Often people are enabled instead of challenged in a healthy way. The apostle John is expressing that we must do more than use words to show real love; we must display it through truthful deeds.

Love is Patience and Understanding

I am not suggesting that we do not give people time to change. Everyone exhibits change at different times and in different ways. What may seem like a small change in the life of one person may seem like a great change in another. When people come with a history of a broken family, dysfunction, or abuse, their change may appear differently than the changes exhibited by others who came from a relatively normal family background. But change, no matter how big or small, is important in God's eyes.

Jesus tells the church of Ephesus in Revelation 2:4 that they had left their first love. He goes on to say repent and do the first works (the things they did earlier). Note that Jesus does not address the church by saying, *First, you must believe correctly and then do what I say.* Why? Because real faith is displayed when we act upon the things which we have already learned. If we stop acting on what we believe, then somewhere along the way we stopped believing.

I think sometimes we look at people in the Bible who experienced moral failures and use that as an excuse to continue in a similar fashion. Take for example, Abram who lied about his wife—not once, but twice to save his own hide (Genesis 20). King Abimelech had taken Abram's wife, but God protected her and blessed Abram and they left the city of Gerar with so many riches that we might think, *Abram lied and God still blessed him, so He can continue to bless me even if I'm lying.* This kind of thinking is faulty. First, we need to remember that God's laws weren't written down at the time of Abram. That doesn't mean that lying wasn't always wrong. It was always God's intention that His laws would be placed in the hearts of men. But first, He had to make a covenant with a people that would accept His rulership. He found Abram to be a man that would put his trust in the true and living God, and blessed him for it. Hebrews 8:10 states, "For this is the covenant that I will make with the house of Israel after those days, says the Lord: I will put My laws in their mind and write them on their hearts; and I will be their God, and they shall be My people."

> **"The grace of God was not given to us so we could sin free of consequence; it was given to us to enable us to overcome sin."**

We are now under the covenant of grace and under the law of Christ, which is an even higher standard of obedience. With regard to lying, Jesus said, "Again you have heard that it was said to those of old, 'You shall not swear falsely, but shall perform your oaths to the Lord.' But I say to you, do not swear at all: neither by heaven, for it is God's throne . . . ." We are held to a higher standard of obedience because it should be emanating from our hearts out of relationship and not simply through law.

Another person we could look at is Rahab the harlot in the book of Joshua. She hid the two spies on the rooftop of her house—while she was running a house of prostitution! God protected her and her whole house when the walls of Jericho fell flat. Does this mean God will bless people if they sleep around? No, that is not what scripture implies. Jesus took sexual sin to a higher level of obedience when he said in Matthew 5:27, "... I say to you that whoever looks at a woman to lust for her has already committed adultery with her in his heart."

The grace of God was not given to us so we could sin free of consequence; it was given to us to enable us to overcome sin. Being under grace does not mean there are no longer "do's and don't's" to consider. The difference is that we have indeed been set free from the law, but we've been freed from being justified by the law. When we respond to the law of Christ through our hearts, it's not for the purpose of justification; it is for the purpose of releasing our faith in what is ours through Christ.

Open the Door

It's true that we cannot break our relationship with God, but we can break our fellowship with Him. If your children disobey you and you send them to their rooms, they're still your children. The act of reprimanding does not cause a break in the relationship, but it causes a change in the fellowship—or the social interaction—with them. The only way fellowship can be broken with God is if we break it, for God is always standing at the door of our hearts desiring to come and enter.

> *Revelation 3:20*
> *"Behold, I stand at the door and knock. If anyone hears My voice and opens the door, I will come in to him and dine with him, and he with Me."*

In the Greek, the verbs for "stand" and "knock" are used in a tense that indicates a continual action. This act describes being out of fellowship with the Lord. I cannot be experiencing intimate fellowship with the Lord if he is always standing at the door knocking.

Let's say you had invited a friend over for dinner and you are waiting for his arrival. You hear the doorbell ring and properly assume it's your friend at the door. You are not face to face with him until you engage in the act of opening the door. Further still, you have not yet experienced a time of conversation and true fellowship until you invite him inside and sit down for dinner. It is the same in the Spirit regarding intimacy with God. I am not saying that if we are out of fellowship with the Lord we are sometimes in the light or in darkness, or that we are in Christ then out of Christ. What I am communicating is that it's possible to be in a place where the benefits of God's grace are not fully functioning in our lives. It all comes down to this: If you find that God is always knocking on the door of your life but never let Him in, then you are not able to fully experience God's absolute best.

Chapter 15
Working Out Your Salvation

I have known so many people who have tried to work for their salvation and ended up very disappointed by their efforts. What we need to do is to learn how to work it out, not work for it. Jesus has provided for us healing, prosperity, and the fruit of the Spirit. We must learn how to work these truths out so that they manifest in our lives. If we place ourselves under the law, we spend our days trying to earn our salvation and that gets wearisome. The good news is that it has already been purchased for us and now what we must do is receive the title deed to it, so to speak.

If we possess this wonderful treasure, then we need to learn how to make a withdrawal. It does very little good to have money in the bank if you don't know how to withdraw from the account and use the funds for your needs.

Philippians 2:12, 13
"Therefore, my beloved, as you have always obeyed, not as in my presence only, but now much more in my absence, work out your own salvation with fear and trembling; for it is God who works in you both to will and to do for His good pleasure."

Notice the previous scripture does not say, *work for your own salvation*. Again, to emphasize it says, "work out your own salvation with fear and trembling."

Whenever we use our faith, we are releasing something we already possess. Let me explain by using the biblical example of the man who was lame for 38 years, found in John 5:4-8. Jesus told this man to rise, take up his bed, and walk. He said this to a man

> "Whenever we use our faith, we are releasing something we already possess."

who, for 38 years, had never been able to simply get up and go for a leisurely stroll. He was never able to get up and help put dishes away. He was never able to just get up and go to work. In those 38 years, he did not possess the ability to simply rise on his own two feet. But after hearing Jesus, faith came and this man knew he had the ability to do what Jesus said, so he stood up. He acted on what he believed. This man received what he desired. Whenever people believe they receive, what they are actually doing is receiving what they already possess. Let's look at another biblical story of healing as an example.

Acts 14:8-10
"And in Lystra a certain man without strength in his feet was sitting, a cripple from his mother's womb, who had never walked. This man heard Paul speaking. Paul, observing him intently and seeing that he had faith to be healed, said with a loud voice, "Stand up straight on your feet!" And he leaped and walked."

Here is a fellow who, for a lifetime, did not possess the strength to stand. But again, once faith came, the ability came with it. One thing I want you to note, however, is that he had to respond to that activated faith for the manifestation to take place. Paul perceived that this man had faith, but if the man had not believed to the point when he tried to stand, he would never have received the full reward of faith. Sometimes we have faith for something, but are not willing to move on it to the degree that we see the full benefits from it. If you are trying to receive from God through your own works, that means you are trying to do it according to your own strength.

Philippians 4:19
"And my God shall supply all your need according to His riches in glory by Christ Jesus."

We often read and speak this verse aloud saying we believe it, but we must read the preceding verses in context to understand to whom this verse applies. Paul is addressing a church who had given in offerings. Paul was telling them that because they released their faith by the act of sowing financially, God would meet all their needs. To understand what I am saying here, let us again consider an illustration of the farmer. A farmer may have seed in his barn, but he will never expect a harvest until he sows the seed in the ground. Why is it that so many believers are expecting a harvest when they have not worked out their salvation by sowing?

Look at the responsibility we have concerning our salvation: it says to work it out with fear and trembling. For years I did not understand this phrase until the Lord spoke to me about it and revealed it to me. The verse is about handling the power of God within your salvation. In Hebrews 2:3 it says, " . . . how shall we escape if we neglect so great a salvation, which at the first began to be spoken by the Lord, and was confirmed to us by those who heard Him . . ." He calls it a great salvation, but what does that term imply?

I have a friend in our church who purchased a car that has 700 horsepower. It's basically a race car made for legal road driving. I was standing there once just looking at it and said, "Let me take it for a drive." My friend said, "I'll let you drive it, but be careful not to put the pedal to the floor or we'll end up on the side of the road!" Working out salvation is similar in that it has great "horsepower under the hood." We must be careful what we say and think, for our salvation provides amazing power and potential within us.

I learned years ago how powerful salvation truly is. The Bible states in Mark 11:24 that if we do not doubt in our hearts but believe the words we say, we can have what we say. This principle works not only in a positive manner, but in a negative manner as well because it is a spiritual principle.

One summer I was in a grocery store and ran into a brother in Christ that I had known for years. During our conversation he had said something to me that really shook me up. He said that God had been so good to him and his family that he was due for some trouble. When he said that, I was instantly grieved in my spirit. Two weeks later his son was killed in a car accident. I am sure he had no idea what he was doing with his mouth, but there are spiritual laws which release good and bad in our lives.

We need to understand that if we say something long enough we will eventually believe it. That belief is then released in our lives. No wonder Paul warned us to work out our salvation with fear and trembling. He understood this spiritual law and the positive and negative effects it could have on us. I am not suggesting we go through life being afraid, but I am saying that we must use the truth God has revealed to us to make our lives bigger and better than they have ever been.

Chapter 16
Motivated by Grace

The grace we receive from God is a great motivator. It is that inward force which enables us to press on through tough circumstances and situations when everything or everyone around us says we should just give up. However, I believe that without proper motivation faith can fail during a time of testing. All of us—if we haven't already—will eventually encounter situations where we must remain highly motivated to endure testing and trials. If our motivation becomes slack, we may regret it.

In order to be properly motivated by grace, we need to understand two very distinct sides of God's nature: His goodness and His severity. Today we hear very little about judgment and repentance. We often hear about the promises of God which are wonderful, but if we don't have a grasp on both sides of God's nature, we can be unbalanced, and that may lead to a fall.

Two Sides of the Coin

Romans 11:19-22
"You will say then, 'Branches were broken off that I might be grafted

in.' Well said. Because of unbelief they were broken off, and you stand by faith. Do not be haughty, but fear. For if God did not spare the natural branches, He may not spare you either. Therefore consider the goodness and severity of God: on those who fell, severity; but toward you, goodness, if you continue in His goodness. Otherwise you also will be cut off."

Consider two sides of a coin: Coins have both heads and tails, but if one side of a coin is marred it is completely unusable. In a similar way, there are two sides to God that must be acknowledged—goodness and severity. Without an awareness of both sides in operation, we will have a difficult time staying motivated by grace.

Leap of Faith

Let's say you're in a high-rise building that's on fire. The Fire Department arrives and lays out a large inflatable mat for you to jump on. The problem is that it's several stories down and you've never jumped out a window before. The fireman is telling you it's safe, but you must jump on your own. You may believe that he's right and that the mat will catch your fall, but it takes a little heat from the fire to burn your backside that motivates you to make the jump. Likewise, sometimes it takes us to feel a little bit of "fire on our backside" to motivate us to jump in and trust God. If you don't have a clear understanding of God's judgment, you may not have what it takes to make the leap and trust Him.

I want to share with you two approaches on how a certain verse can be taught. You'll discover one teaching is lacking something important and can bring with it misunderstanding.

Suppose I'm teaching on tithing and giving, and I refer to the text in Malachi 3:10 which states:

"Bring all the tithes into the storehouse,
That there may be food in My house,
And try Me now in this,"
Says the Lord of hosts,
"If I will not open for you the windows of heaven
And pour out for you such blessing
That there will not be room enough to receive it.

And I will rebuke the devourer for your sakes,
So that he will not destroy the fruit of your ground"

From there I proceed by saying that God doesn't curse New Testament believers but I emphasize that God says He'll pour out blessings in your life to the degree that if you own a two-bedroom home, He can give you double that and He'll rebuke the devourer for you so that the appliances in your home will last and your vehicle won't break down and on and on. While the blessing of God is true, what happens if I don't teach on what's "on the other side of the coin"? If you don't obey God concerning tithes and offerings, there is going to be a curse upon your life. God hasn't put a curse upon you, but because sin is still in operation, the world is still under a curse. Think of it like a rainy day. To get out from under the rain, you need an umbrella for protection. In this case the curse upon the world is like the rain, and obeying in faith is like the umbrella.

God will allow negative consequences into our lives if we don't obey Him. The Bible states that "many are the afflictions of the righteous" (Psalm 34:19), therefore, I don't need to unnecessarily add more trouble to my own life by being in disobedience. Because God is just, He must allow consequences in our lives if we open the door to them through our own willing disobedience.

Now let's take the scripture Proverbs 10:22 for examination. It says, "The blessing of the Lord makes one rich, and He adds no sorrow with it." The truth is you can prosper if you work long hours and sacrifice time with your family and compromise in other areas. But that's the point: prospering in this manner will cost you and your loved ones something dear. When we prosper according to God's design, He brings it about in ways that will not cost us our marriage or hurt our kids or other relationships.

Here's another example which is found in Matthew 18:21-35, which is the parable of the unforgiving servant. Jesus tells about a servant who owed a debt to his master and begged for mercy. As an act of compassion, the master released the servant and forgave him of his debt. Now the servant had come across someone who had owed him, yet the servant was unmerciful and unforgiving of the debt that was due. In the parable, Jesus said that the master had heard of this, became angry with that servant and gave him over to the torturers until all was paid. Then Jesus addressed the crowd and said, "So My heavenly Father also will do to you if each of you, from his heart, does not forgive his brother his trespasses." Clearly, we will endure a consequence if we don't forgive from our heart. I don't know what it means to be handed over to the torturers, but I'll forgive even when it's hard, because I can feel a little fire on my back!

Understanding Divine Judgment

As I've mentioned earlier, it seems like very few people speak on the judgment of God these days. I think that's largely due in part to the difficulty of tying grace and judgment together. I think people have a hard time with that. Just because we don't speak on judgment does not mean God will not enforce spiritual truth in our life. (Just because no one's talking about the new traffic camera at your intersection doesn't mean you won't get a ticket if you run a red light at that stop either!)

Some people believe there is no longer any kind of judgment on the church because God has judged our sins by laying it on the body of Jesus at the cross. Before we agree with that line of thinking, let's examine what the scriptures say about this matter.

> *Hebrews 13:4*
> *"Marriage is honorable among all, and the bed undefiled; but fornicators and adulterers God will judge."*

> *1 Corinthians 11:31-32*
> *"For if we would judge ourselves, we would not be judged. But when we are judged, we are chastened by the Lord, that we may not be condemned with the world."*

> *1 Peter 4:17*
> *"For the time has come for judgment to begin at the house of God; and if it begins with us first, what will be the end of those who do not obey the gospel of God?"*

Divine judgment is designed to position us for success and prevent a negative outcome toward which we could be headed.

The Seven Churches

The Lord showed me something about the seven churches in the book of

Revelation. I noticed that all the churches had one thing in common: Jesus judged the works of the church. Only one did not lack in anything, but the other six fell short in some areas. Another aspect that caught my attention was that there was no mention of sin even though their actions within the churches were sinful. The reason for this is because as believers in Jesus Christ, God doesn't judge our sins, only our works. The Bible states in Romans 14:23 that "whatever is not from faith is sin," so the Lord judges our works according to the Word in order that we might receive a reward in this life, and also an eternal one in the life to come.

In the book of Revelation, the church of Ephesus is told that they have left their first love. Jesus then reminds them to do the things they did in the beginning. He goes on to say that that those who overcome will partake from the tree of life. He warns the church that if they do not do well, their lampstand will be removed. This isn't a threat of punishment, but a warning that they could lose the blessing they had obtained since salvation.

Mark 4:24
"Take heed what you hear. With the same measure you use, it will be measured to you; and to you who hear, more will be given. For whoever has, to him more will be given; but whoever does not have, even what he has will be taken away from him."

This scripture shows us that it is possible to lose rewards based on not doing those things which God has instructed us to do. Our salvation is not what is at stake here, but the possibility of blessing and reward.

In chapter 11 of this book we discussed what will happen at the judgment seat of Christ according to 1 Corinthians 3:11-17. (Also, read 2 Corinthians 5:10.) To reiterate, at that time of judgment what will be judged are works. If motives are right, an eternal reward will be given; it will not be judgment of sin.

Hebrews 9:28
"...so Christ was offered once to bear the sins of many. To those who eagerly wait for Him He will appear a second time, apart from sin, for salvation."

Note in the above verse that Jesus will appear a second time to believers "apart from sin." In a similar way, God judges us in this life. The difference is that in this life His Word corrects us, and we have the opportunity to make the changes necessary to maintain our blessing and to secure our eternal rewards to come. When we stand before the judgment seat of Christ, there will no longer be time to make those changes. We will be rewarded purely based on what we had done on earth.

Getting the Most Out of Grace

My wife loves to save money, and because of that, she knows how to maximize the use of most everything. She'll take a ketchup bottle, turn it upside down and cut off the top in order to get the last drop out of it. She'll do something similar with toothpaste as well. She'll twist that tube up so tight in order to push all the toothpaste toward the opening that I think it might explode. She does this because she doesn't want to waste the value of anything that could be put to good use. If you love to get a good deal when you shop, you'll be attracted to special sales, clearances, and coupons. You want to find ways to maximize your funds so that you get the most out of your spending.

Now, let's discuss the difference between fans and spectators as they relate to sports. Fans learn everything about the game they love—they know the players' names, their position, maybe even all of their statistics. They have a great enthusiasm regarding their team's games. If they attend one, they may even paint their faces in their team's colors and jump up and down wildly, yelling and screaming with each and every play made. A spectator of a game will do none of that. Sure, they may cheer when a good play happens, but if they're simply spectating, they're only "into it" temporarily; they are not motivated beyond the moment.

In order to maximize all the benefits of grace, we must understand the value of it. When we understand that, we will do what we can to receive all that's available to us. If we are going to get the most out of grace, then we'll also need to be "fans" of Jesus, not just "spectators." We need to have a passion and an enthusiasm for him and not just be motivated by the moment. Most importantly, in order to receive the most benefit from our faith, we must be motivated by love. It is the same way with grace.

Enjoying All of It

I have heard people say things like, *I just love the Word, but I'm not really into singing during service.* But here's the issue: The Word of God is to help us, but praise and worship is for God. When I'm preaching a message, there is nothing I can say that surprises God or comes as news to Him. But the portion of the service that really blesses Him the most is when we are singing His praises and coming together in worship.

Getting back to our fan analogy—real fans don't care when the game is over; in fact they love it when it goes into overtime. In a similar way, "real fans" of Jesus do not head for the exit door when the altar call is made. Fans also endure all kinds of weather to support their team; they don't look for excuses as to why they can't show up. To be very honest with you, they aren't like some Christians who look outside on a Sunday morning and say, *Well, it looks like it might snow. I'm staying home. Better play it safe.* The Bible encourages us to be together in fellowship, especially when times seem tough.

> *Hebrews 10:25*
> *"...not forsaking the assembling of ourselves together, as is the manner of some, but exhorting one another, and so much the more as you see the Day approaching."*

I like how this verse emphasizes that we should be even closer as a church body as we see the Last Days approaching. We should not only desire to be with one another in fellowship, but we should, as a body of believers, desire to be together in the presence of our Lord Jesus. One of the things I love most about Jesus is being in his presence. The more we experience him, the more we desire him. We begin to yearn for his presence in our lives as something we cannot live without. King David wrote about this kind of desire to be with the Lord, saying, "As the deer pants for the water brooks, so pants my soul for You, O God." This type of thirst that David wrote about is significant because he was describing not only a need, but a great desire. The word David used for "deer" was female, not a buck. The reason we can know David was describing a great thirst for God was because of the use of this word. Bucks have antlers and their horns work like radiators during their period of growth, giving them a way to cool themselves, but the females are not equipped with this cooling system; thus they are much thirstier than the males. David took what he could see was true in nature and applied that to describe his thirst for God.

Use the Truth Correctly

It is possible to receive fewer benefits from the grace provided to us by misusing truth. If we use truth the way God intended and designed, we would receive the benefits of grace to greater degrees. A simple illustration or two can really communicate what I think is important to understand here. If you tried to eat with a screwdriver instead of a fork, you might get a little food in your mouth, but you wouldn't be extremely successful at eating your meal. You wouldn't use a toothbrush to comb your hair because that would be ineffective (not to mention weird). If we use God's Word and His truth properly, we will truly be able to access His promises, protection, and blessings in greater ways. Let's take a look at the following verse concerning this.

> *John 8:31, 32*
> *"Then Jesus said to those Jews who believed Him, "If you abide in My word, you are My disciples indeed. And you shall know the truth, and the truth shall make you free."*

What does it mean to be free? Does it mean that we can do whatever we want to do, or are we free in a different sense? God loved us so much that He removed condemnation, guilt, and fear from our lives by putting Jesus on the cross. He loved us so much that He rescued us from the very things that caused us to be bound to sin. Romans 8:2 says, "the law of the Spirit of life in Christ Jesus has made me free from the law of sin and death." Why does Paul use the words "the law of sin and death"? It describes how the consequences of sin were released into our lives when Adam and Eve had sinned; they died spiritually and both were condemned. Guilt began to empower the flesh in their lives. When we believed that Jesus had forgiven us of all our sins, God had released us from the spirit of condemnation. Many have taken this truth—that we are now no longer condemned—and have mishandled and misused it in such a way that has made it difficult for others to understand God's intention in being free in Christ.

Diluting the Truth

This is a true, biblical statement: We are saved by grace through faith, not by works. However, I believe many who have heard the message of grace have only listened to parts they wanted to hear, and shut their ears to the harder parts of the message of grace. If you have followed the flow over the last 20 years of the church, you can see how this partiality in hearing has crept into the lifestyle of much of the church. I remember the first time I heard this approach to what I'll call "diluted truth." I heard a preacher telling the congregation that for those who did not tithe in his church to begin giving at whatever level they could, and then believe God to give them enough to reach the ten percent. As soon as the preacher had said that, I thought to myself, *That would be like a cheating husband coming home and telling his wife that he's repenting of his unfaithfulness, and that he'll cut back his extramarital activities to only a few times a month until he's able to completely cut off the affair.*

Let's look at a biblical example of this "partial hearing." The story involves Cain and Abel.

Genesis 4:2-7
"Now Abel was a keeper of sheep, but Cain was a tiller of the ground. And in the process of time it came to pass that Cain brought an offering of the fruit of the ground to the Lord. Abel also brought of the firstborn of his flock and of their fat. And the Lord respected Abel and his offering, but He did not respect Cain and his offering. And Cain was very angry, and his countenance fell. So the Lord said to Cain, "Why are you angry? And why has your countenance fallen? If you do well, will you not be accepted? And if you do not do well, sin lies at the door. And its desire is for you, but you should rule over it."

> **"Just because we are under grace does not mean obedience is optional."**

We can conclude that Abel was tithing and Cain was not. The scripture cites that Abel had brought the firstborn of his flock to the Lord, and his offering was accepted. This is not the case for Cain, whose offering was not respected by God. The text is even more severe, showing that God did not even have respect toward Cain himself. Yet the Lord encouraged Cain by telling him that he would be accepted if he were to do well. God made it very clear through this exchange that we are acceptable when we do what is right. You might be thinking, 'How does that apply to New Testament believers, to those who are under grace?' Well, it is true that under grace you won't go to hell if you don't tithe, but the truth of the matter is that you will not receive the full benefits of the blessing which comes with the blessing of Abraham. Just because we are under grace does not mean obedience is optional. The definition of the word "optional" means *to be left up to one's own choice; not required or mandated.* When the scriptures are clear on a matter, or when the truth of scripture has been revealed to our hearts, we ought to take it as a command and not an option.

I was shocked the other day to hear a preacher say that tithing was not a requirement for today. It's true that it's not required in order to go to heaven, but it is required to increase finances in your life. Tithing is a spiritual principle. The preacher attempted to prove his point by looking at the text of Hebrews 7:12 which says, "For the priesthood being changed, of necessity there is also a change of the law." This preacher was trying to prove there was no more law regarding tithing, but if you examine the verse in context, it explains that under the law the priests must come from the tribe of Levi. The writer of Hebrews reveals the new covenant had different rules and that Jesus' ministry was after the order of Melchizedek who was a king and a priest, just like Jesus. It was Abraham who first tithed to Melchizedek who is a type of the Lord Jesus and carries on with this priesthood. The point I'm making is this: Just because we are under grace does not mean God no longer requires anything from us in order to help us bear spiritual, eternal fruit.

No Fruit is Death

When we are saved by grace, we will always produce fruit. No matter the quantity, those who are saved will bear fruit in their lives. If a person shows no fruit at all, then he or she would really need to examine whether a salvation experience had taken place. In chapter 2 of this book, we briefly touched on the parable of the talents found in Matthew 25. We know that the master left the servants in charge of his money for the purpose of bringing increase to the master himself. Clearly, the master in the parable represents God the Father and the servants represent us, God's stewards. The wicked and lazy servant, the one who buried his talent in the ground in the parable represents one who does not produce fruit for the kingdom. That servant was cast into outer darkness. I don't think that's describing the shady side of heaven. If we profess to be truly saved, we will be producing fruit for God's kingdom.

Chapter 17
Grace Feeds Determination

Through the years I have discovered that sometimes it's difficult to know what to do or where to turn for direction, even while walking with God. This feeling of uncertainty can be especially frustrating when faith is really needed to overcome a trying time. Having a determined kind of faith is one quality that helps us all to start heading in a proper direction. I also believe that having resolve or determination is a trait that everyone needs in order to put works to their faith. We must be determined in order for our faith to bring about the things we desire.

The kind of determination that sees dreams come to pass, goals realized, and prayers answered is what I would call a winning determination. Let me describe to you what I'm talking about. A winning determination is the kind of determination that, when facing a trial, it actually increases as the situation gets rougher. The harder your problem pushes you, the more you push back or resist the problem. The more you feel squeezed by your situation, the greater your resistance becomes. That is winning determination, and that is the kind of determination that accompanies real faith. In essence, it is what the Bible calls perseverance.

In the Bible, the word perseverance is made by combining two Greek words, *pro,* meaning *towards* and *karteros*, meaning *strong*. It quite literally means *to be strong toward something.* Whenever people fall short or give up on a dream or desire, it's not because of a lack of opportunity or lack of education or talent, but what I believe is a lack of determination, or perseverance, in their lives.

With this in mind, let's look at a parable that Jesus shared.

Luke 18:1-8
"Then He spoke a parable to them, that men always ought to pray and not lose heart, saying: "There was in a certain city a judge who did not fear God nor regard man. Now there was a widow in that city; and she came to him, saying, 'Get justice for me from my adversary.' And he would not for a while; but afterward he said within himself, 'Though I do not fear God nor regard man, yet because this widow troubles me I will avenge her, lest by her continual coming she weary me.'"

Then the Lord said, "Hear what the unjust judge said. And shall God not avenge His own elect who cry out day and night to Him, though He bears long with them? I tell you that He will avenge them speedily. Nevertheless, when the Son of Man comes, will He really find faith on the earth?"

For years I did not understand this parable. I had thought that if you asked for something over and over again it must be due to unbelief, because Mark 11:24 says to believe that you receive and that you will have what you ask. I missed the point of the parable which is really talking about determination in our prayers. This scripture is not telling us how to believe, but how to pray with determination. The parable is also not talking about the workings of faith, but it is stressing that we should never give up in our prayers. The unjust judge in the story continued to tell the woman "no," but eventually granted her request because of her extreme determination.

Possessing determination can be compared to the potential you have within your talent. Many people have great undeveloped talent within them, but it is refined with determination. You would never hear a beautiful song without the artist's determination to develop it. Sometimes it takes years for a talent to be developed to its maximum potential, but it is only honed through sheer determination; an unwillingness to never give up.

Now, concerning faith, we will never do all the things God desires for us to do if we don't stir up determination to believe and never give up. If we lose heart and surrender during the hard times, faith cannot succeed.

Luke 17:5-6
"And the apostles said to the Lord, "Increase our faith." So the Lord said, "If you have faith as a mustard seed, you can say to this mulberry tree, 'Be pulled up by the roots and be planted in the sea,' and it would obey you."

In the above scripture, the Greek word used for "if" indicates that the sentence is a first-class sentence, which, if you remember from an earlier explanation, it is a kind of sentence that assumes the information is true. Plus, it is also in the imperfect tense, which denotes a continuous, ongoing, or repeated action. Basically, Jesus is telling the disciples that they have the mustard seed and what they must do to increase their faith is to continue to remain determined and speak words of faith.

The Harder You Push

The devil is fully aware that the harder he tries to defeat you, the more it could cause a backfire on him. He's aware that you may become more resolute with each attack or provocation. When the devil attacks you, he knows that he has a lot to lose if he isn't successful in keeping you down. Sometimes we may feel like giving in and giving up, but if we have the heart to remain persistent just a little longer, we might just receive the breakthrough we need. Sometimes we just need to seek God a little longer, or pray one more time in earnest faith. Sometimes we need to just pursue that dream once more in order to see it fulfilled.

We can only become stronger during a struggle if we change our level of determination in the fight. When rough times come and we don't adjust our level of determination to make it through, it will be easy to give up. There are times when we must really take command of our problems and demand it to come under control. When you're looking to jump over an obstacle, sometimes you need to back up so you can gain more momentum to overtake it. In the same way spiritually, sometimes we need to "back up" so we can get a good run at the situation. Whether we feel we need to back up, start fresh, or try again, determination will not allow us to give up during a time of trial and testing. Let's look at this type of determination in action from the story of Jacob, just before the Lord named him Israel.

Genesis 32:24-26
"Then Jacob was left alone; and a Man wrestled with him until the breaking of day. Now when He saw that He did not prevail against him, He touched the socket of his hip; and the socket of Jacob's hip was out of joint as He wrestled with him. And He said, "Let Me go, for the day breaks." But he said, "I will not let You go unless You bless me!"

Jacob was so determined to receive God's blessing that he wouldn't release the angel of the Lord, even while he was in incredible pain. Think of wrestling with a hip out of joint! Jacob's refusal to give up allowed God to bless him. Now listen to what I'm about to say to you personally: You may not feel as if you're qualified or capable to do what God has put in your heart to accomplish, but stay determined, stick with what you know to do, and eventually you will succeed.

Another example of determination that encourages me is Caleb's story. In Numbers 13 we find Moses choosing the twelve spies to survey the land which God had promised them. After their forty-day mission, only Caleb and Joshua returned with a good report, saying that they could overtake the people who dwelled there. We know that the Israelites did not enter the promised land at that time because of their lack of faith, refusing to believe God for victory. Caleb was not sentenced to die in the wilderness along with the older generation and remained strong, able, and determined for 40 years in order to possess the land God had promised them. Caleb was about 45 years old at the time God laid judgment on the Israelites, yet he remained resolved to possess God's promise at 85 years old. Caleb not only came to possess the land, but was able to enjoy the fruits of his labor and was blessed for his faith. He was still fired up and burning strong for God after all those years. He hadn't lowered his standards or lost his resolve at all.

As a final example, I want you to consider the determination of this woman who we considered earlier, a woman who ended up receiving a "long-distance miracle."

Matthew 15:21-28
"Then Jesus went out from there and departed to the region of Tyre and Sidon. And behold, a woman of Canaan came from that region and cried out to Him, saying, "Have mercy on me, O Lord, Son of David! My daughter is severely demon-possessed."But He answered her not a word. And His disciples came and urged Him, saying, "Send her away, for she cries out after us."But He answered and said, "I was not sent except to the lost sheep of the house of Israel."Then she came and worshiped Him, saying, "Lord, help me!"But He answered and said, "It is not good to take the children's bread and throw it to the little dogs."And she said, "Yes, Lord, yet even the little dogs eat the crumbs which fall from their masters' table."Then Jesus answered and said to her, "O woman, great is your faith! Let it be to you as you desire." And her daughter was healed from that very hour."

This woman was so determined to receive from the Lord that she would not take "no" for an answer. Jesus' own disciples tried turning her away, but they became so frustrated with her that they asked Jesus to handle the situation. I want you to note how she responded to the Lord who told her it was not yet time for her miracle. Another point to note in this story is that this woman came to Jesus under "false pretenses." She was not a Jew nor a religious woman, but gave the appearance of one by calling Jesus "Son of David." This was a term used specifically by the Jews. Jesus uncovered this by using the metaphorical term "dog" to refer to her. This was a term that was used at that time to describe ungodly people. In spite of all this, she was so determined in her need that she refused to leave without a miracle. Most people would be offended but she was willing to have her true character revealed if it resulted in healing for her daughter. My friend, how determined are you to receive the miracle you need? Are you determined enough to let down your guard and allow yourself to be fully exposed by Jesus? In the end, we can see that this woman was blessed and received her "long-distance" miracle, for Jesus had never even laid a hand on her daughter, yet was fully restored.

Hebrews 11:6
"But without faith it is impossible to please Him, for he who comes to God must believe that He is, and that He is a rewarder of those who diligently seek Him."

I personally believe one of the ways Satan prevents us from receiving

God's best is by distracting our focus. I don't believe that Satan knows our future, but I think he has good indicators that allow him to sense when God is about to promote someone spiritually, or about to speak something to them that is life-altering. I believe it is during these times when the enemy desperately attempts to get you to disobey the Lord—especially in small ways—to keep you from that blessing.

If you want to go to the next level in your life, examine where you are and increase that determination if you find it has been lacking. I am amazed at how easily some people give up on their dream. If they don't get what they want in the time they want it, some just decide to halt their pursuit. Stay on course and don't let circumstances move you. Remain in faith and keep your eyes fixed on the One who desires to see you succeed.

The more we grasp God's grace toward us, the more we are able to love Him. There is something so wonderful about responding to His love in our lives. Responding to this amazing grace causes us to be true worshipers of God. It removes the effort out of obeying and serving Him. As we discussed earlier about reaction versus response, it is one thing to do something out of obligation. It something else entirely to simply desire to worship the Lord because of all He has done on our behalf. This is true worship. I believe that understanding these truths of grace will create within you an intense desire to be pleasing to God and will set you on course into His perfect will.

Grace is like the wind in a sail. When the sail is full of wind, all you have to do is set your course and the wind pushes you along. Grace is truly freeing and is wonderful empowerment. It takes the burden out of doing what He commands. It is my prayer that from this point and beyond, you will never be the same again. I pray that your service to and worship of God will stem forth out of His great love toward you, and that you will continue to walk in the blessing of His grace and be continually amazed by His love.

Special Invitation

If you are not yet a follower of Jesus but you desire to be, I ask that you would pray this prayer.

Heavenly Father, I believe that Jesus came to die for my sins. I believe you rose him from the dead for my benefit, and I confess him as Lord over my life. I declare today that Jesus is my Lord and I will follow him for the rest of my life. Thank you. In Jesus' Name I pray, Amen.

If you have just prayed this prayer, it is my honor to welcome you to the family of God. Ask God to help you find a church, and begin to plug in and grow with the saints. Above all, I pray that your latter days may be better than your former days. I believe that because you have read this book, you desire to abide in the right place with God. There is great power in simply abiding in His presence, and God wants nothing more than for you to experience all He has prepared for you—in this life, and in the one yet to come.